A Christian Educator's Book of Lists

A Christian Educator's Book of Lists

israel galindo

SMYTH&HELWYS
PUBLISHING, INCORPORATED   MACON, GEORGIA

Smyth & Helwys Publishing, Inc.
6316 Peake Road
Macon, Georgia 31210-3960
1-800-747-3016
©2003 by Smyth & Helwys Publishing

The paper used in this publication meets the minimum requirements of American National
Standard for Information Sciences—Permanence
of Paper for Printed Library Materials.
ANSI Z39.48–1984. (alk. paper)

Library of Congress Cataloging-in-Publication Data

Galindo, Israel.
    Help! a Christian educator's book of lists /
    by Israel Galindo.
    p. cm.
    Includes bibliographical references and index.
    ISBN 1-57312-347-1 (alk. paper)
    1. Christian education—Miscellanea.
    I. Title.
    BV1471.3 G35 2002
    268—dc21

                                                2002151750
                                                CIP

Table of Contents

Bible and History

Books, Journals, and Resources

Educational Foundations

Personal Growth and Professional Survival

Programs

Teaching and Instruction

Tools of the Trade

Miscellaneous

This one is for Barbara, Doug, and Tom,
who are on the "top of my list."

Acknowledgments

Special thanks to the following friends and colleagues who contributed ideas and lists to help make this work more useful: Sanford Beckett, Vicki Blose, Timothy Brock, Robert Dibble, Marty Canaday, David Deakle, Mike Harton, Patricia Morgan, Jack Price, Kathy Kessler Price, Mark Price, Gregory Randall. ∎

Introduction

Have you ever needed a piece of information that you weren't sure where to find? Did you ever lose an hour tracking down basic information because you didn't remember where you filed it? Has a Sunday school teacher ever asked you, "Which came first, the Book of Esther or the Battle of Sennacherib?" and all you could do was respond with a blank stare? Have you ever been asked to give an impromptu lecture and felt your brain freeze? Have you ever wondered who were the best Christian educators of the century? This resource may be for you.

I've often found myself during a typical workweek needing to access a basic piece of information—either for developing course material, answering a student's question, or trying to help someone during a telephone conversation. Of course, that information is spread among various books on library shelves or buried somewhere in a filing system. Eventually I acquired the habit of carrying a file of frequently-used lists in my electronic handheld PIM (personal information manager). But often I've wished for a single source of basic information and collected wisdom upon which to draw.

It is my hope that this book will help fill that need by providing basic information and collected wisdom Christian educators and teachers should have available. For experienced Christian educators and teachers, this book serves as a reminder of what they already know. For novice church educators, this book provides suggestions on where to begin pursuing more in-depth information on a wide range of subjects. At the heart of this book is the desire to make available to churches and their leaders a handbook of basic, practical information for effective Christian education. Part encyclopedia, part trivia resource, part practical "how to" compilations, part teaching manual, and part general knowledge index, the book is a handy reference tool for every church educator.

Administration

Administrative Functions of the Christian Educator
- Enlistment and development of church educators
- Budget development
- Planning, development, and maintenance of educational programs
- Training and supervision of paid and volunteer staff
- Coordinating educational resources (budget, time, personnel, physical plant)
- Leadership in key educational and ministry committees, teams, and groups
- Maintenance of vital records related to educational ministry

Administrative Meeting Agenda (Sample)
1. Prayer
2. Reading and call for acceptance of minutes
3. Pastor's or moderator's report
4. Financial report
5. Program areas reports
6. Committee reports
7. Old business
8. New business
9. Review and assign actions to be taken
10. Close

Blunders, Common Administrative
- Lack of clarity in vision and mission
- Lack of sufficient or realistic planning
- Lack of on-going mission- and values-centered goals and objectives

- Lack of supervision of staff, personnel, participants, or players
- Lack of honesty with people and constituents
- Lack of practicing the courage of convictions
- Lack of attention to resources and budgeting
- Lack of clear decision-making procedures and philosophy
- Lack of honest evaluation
- Lack of clear communication with constituents
- Lack of congruency between responsibility and authority
- Lack of intentional organizational oversight (budget, policies, procedures)

Church Governance, Types of

Congregational (Baptist, Congregational, Lutheran)
Episcopal (Anglican, Episcopal, Lutheran)
Apostolic (Monarchial, Roman Catholic)
Presbyterian (Calvinist, Presbyterian)

Church Growth

Types of Numerical Growth

1. *Biological*–those born into member families and baptized into membership
2. *New converts*–new believers from non-churched backgrounds
3. *Transfer of membership*–those joining from other churches or denominations
4. *Transitional memberships*–those joining the church for predetermined period of time or purposes

Signs of a Stagnant Congregation

1. Dwelling on the past glory days
2. Lack of intentional plan for growth
3. Uninformed membership
4. Criticism of leadership and staff
5. Control group(s) and decision-makers comprised of "old guard"
6. Overemphasis on resource conservation
7. High dependence on paid staff
8. Perpetual anxiety over finances

9. Neglect of physical plant
10. Generational gaps in membership (young adults, young families)

Conflict, Types of Church

Doctrinal
Personality
Leadership
Organizational
Justice
Cultural
Moral
Financial
Generalized anxiety

Congregations, Life Stages of

1. Establishment and Organization Stage
    "Birth," incorporation
    Dependent on founding members and/or pastor
    Vision-oriented
2. Formation Stage
    Early development
    Systemic identity dynamics form
    Systemic emotional systems form
3. Development Stage
    "Adolescence"
    Programs development
    Core groups patterned
    Corporate values formation
4. Plateau Stage
    May happen in adolescence through maturity
    Homeostatic forces a primary dynamic
5. Second Development Stage
    Re-visioning
    Struggle toward growth
6. Survival and Decline Stage

If capacity for re-visioning and resilience are not present in the corporate identity, the church may move toward decline and eventual death. The congregation needs to handle internal and external deficit forces well in order to move back to a new (third) development stage.

Families, Life Stages of

1. Married Couples (without Children)
2. Childbearing families (oldest child is birth-30 months)
3. Families with preschool children (oldest child is 30 months–6 years)
4. Families with school children (oldest child is 6-13 years)
5. Families with teenagers (oldest child is 13-20 years)
6. Families as launching centers (first child gone to last child leaving home)
7. Middle-aged parents (empty nest to retirement)
8. Aging family members (retirement/death of both spouses)

Functions of a Church

1. Worship (Praise)
2. Witness (Proclamation)
3. Education (Discipleship)
4. Ministry (Missions, Service)
5. Fellowship (Community)

Group Problem-Solving Process

1. Identify the problem.
2. Gather information.
3. Clarify the problem and define the issue the group will address.
4. Determine decision-making process (vote, consensus, delegation).
5. Explore alternative solutions (brainstorm, listen).
6. Evaluate best possible alternative solutions and anticipate outcomes.
7. Decide on the solution approach.
8. Assign roles and responsibilities.
9. Determine deadline for actions.
10. Summarize problem, decision, and actions.
11. Provide for feedback and evaluation of actions.

Group Process Functions

1. Group formation
2. Group organization
3. Group membership decisions: expectations, roles, and tenure?
4. Group decision-making processes: vote? consensus? fiat?
5. Group control and direction: Who's in charge and were are we going?
6. Group information processing: Who gathers information?
7. Balance of process roles: initiating, seeking consensus, summarizing, challenging, clarifying, compromising, relieving tension, encouraging
8. Group values and culture: dependence/independence; reciprocity; level of trust; level of commitment; confidentiality; openness

Hiring Staff

Job Description Outline (Sample)
Position title
Hiring process datelines
Position summary
Position duties
Position specifications
    Education or training required
    Ordination or certification required
    Experience required
    Physical demands of the job
    Supervision
    Working conditions
    Background check if required
    Responsibilities specific to job

Steps to Hiring Staff
1. Determine the need for the position.
2. Review policies related to hiring and supervision of staff (congregational vote needed?).
3. Determine the scope of the position (full-time; part-time; specialization).

4. Determine financial package.
5. Budget for the position.
6. Seek the best person for the job; professional, academic, personal qualifications.
7. Publish job description, timetable for hire, and hiring process.
8. Involve individuals and groups affected by the hire.
9. Accept applications.
10. Check and double-check references.
11. Set up interview process.
12. Make decision and invitation to hire.
13. Follow up with all applicants.
14. Establish formal orientation process for new hire.

Steps to Dismissing Staff
1. Discuss situation thoroughly with Senior Pastor and/or administrator.
2. Review church policies on staff dismissal process.
3. Discuss matter with Personnel Committee and present recommendation for action. Review personnel documentation and set date for dismissal.
4. Supervisor and member of Personnel Committee meet with the staff in question to present decision, review terms, and answer questions.
5. Arrange to have last paycheck ready for dismissal day.

Leadership Styles
1. Autocratic
• Firm control and authority is an issue.
• Seldom consults others on decisions.
• Orders are given to be followed to the letter.
• Leader has total responsibility for results.
• Will not delegate authority lightly
• Tends to be aggressive

2. Democratic
• Relies on group decisions

- Guides work of groups and makes good delegation of responsibility
- Group helps formulate policy.
- Leader may be perceived as weak.
- Leader usually feels secure in job.

3. Laissez-faire
- Provides vision
- Functions as a resource person when needed
- Workers are left on their own within their responsibilities
- Needs constituents who are mature, self-motivated, and need little supervision
- Leader susceptible to sabotage from immature or willful people

4. Paternalistic
- Identification between leader and constituents enmeshed
- Leadership tends to be well meaning but weak.
- Family style decision-making processes
- Discipline is difficult to maintain.

5. Managerial
- Leader functions as CEO.
- Stress on efficiency
- Task- and results-oriented
- Leader works out of policies and procedures.

Management Process
- Planning (Programs)
- Organizing (Administration)
- Motivation (Leadership)
- Controlling (Supervision)

Office Forms to Have On-Hand
- Accident Report
- Application Interview
- Application Reference Check
- Books Borrowed

- Building Key Sign-out
- Building Maintenance & Repair Request
- Building Use Application
- Check Requisition
- Computer System(s) Backup Schedule Checklist
- Fax Cover
- Hospital and Shut-ins Visitation
- I-9 Employment Eligibility Verification
- Inventory
- Membership Transfer Request
- New Employee Orientation Checklist
- Preschool Area Sign-in/Sign-out
- Purchase Order Request
- Staff Vacation Sign-up
- Tax Exempt Status Letter
- Telephone Message ("While you were out")
- To-do List
- Usher's Sunday Service(s) Attendance and Incidents
- Vacation Request
- W-4 & W-2

Operating Documents for the Church

1. Church Covenant
2. Church Constitution and By-laws
3. Statement of Policies
   a. Hiring and dismissal
   b. Personnel
      (1) Salary and pay scale
      (2) Vacation and sabbatical
      (3) Clergy misconduct
   c. Building use
   d. Business meetings
   e. Membership
   f. Budgeting and finances
   g. Church officers and elections
   h. Weddings and funerals

4. Articles of Faith
5. Articles of Incorporation
6. Church Budget (should be considered a "theological document")

Organization, Principles of

1. Provide clear objectives.
2. Coordinate actions, tasks, and goals.
3. Consolidate specializations (avoid duplication of efforts and resources).
4. Facilitate focus of leadership (who is in charge?).
5. Maintain locus of control (who is ultimately responsible?).
6. Ensure that authority and responsibility are congruent.
7. Delegate to furthest level.
8. Flatten span of control (supervise as few organizational "levels" as possible).
9. Provide structure and processes for efficient communication.
10. Maintain balance of purpose (avoid special interests not consistent with the vision and mission of the organization).

Planning, Principles of

1. Maintain clarity about issues related to identity, purpose, mission, and function.
2. Identify need(s) and/or vision.
3. Articulate goals and objectives.
4. Identify resources and assets to achieving goals.
5. Prioritize needs and action steps.
6. Identify current and potential limitations and inhibitors achieving goals; anticipate problems and their solutions.
7. Invite and facilitate broad participation in the planning process.
8. Assign responsibilities, accountability, and authority related to actions.
9. Establish new pathways of communication for the planning processes.
10. Do not over-plan—move ahead when enough elements are in place to begin action steps and be flexible enough to adapt to changing situations, surprises, and unanticipated obstacles.
11. Establish evaluation processes and checkpoints.

Time-Wasters to Avoid

- Inefficiency in executing tasks
- Indecision (When information is lacking and unobtainable, or when pros and cons are in balance, *any* decision is better than none.)
- Anxiety
- Environment that hinders work (messy desk and unorganized office)
- Communication systems that hinder maintaining open channels of dialogue and information
- Junk mail (throw it out)
- Junk e-mail (delete it)
- Salespeople making a "cold call" (politely hang up or refuse to see them)
- Meetings with no agenda or clearly defined purpose
- "Drop-in" visits (politely encourage them to make an appointment)

Bible and History

Apocrypha
Additions to Esther
Baruch
Bel and the Dragon
First Book of Esdras
Second Book of Esdras
Judith
Epistle of Jeremiah
First Book of the Maccabees
Second Book of the Maccabees
Third Book of the Maccabees
Fourth Book of the Maccabees
Prayer of Manasseh
Psalm 151
Ecclesiasticus (or Sirach)
Prayer of Azariah
Song of the Three Young Men
Susanna
Tobit
Wisdom of Solomon

Chronology, Bible Events (approximate dating)
BC (BCE)
2000   Age of the Patriarchs (Abraham, Isaac, Jacob)
1700   Sojourn into Egypt (Joseph)
1400   Exodus and conquest of Canaan (Moses, Ten
       Commandments, Joshua)

1200   Period of the Judges
1020   Saul becomes King of Israel
1000   Davidic Kingdom
961   Solomon and first temple
922   Divided Kingdom: Israel in North, Judah in South
783   King Uzziah in the Southern Kingdom
721   Kingdom of Israel falls to Assyria
587   Kingdom of Judah falls to Babylonia; temple destroyed
538   Jews return to Jerusalem and rebuild temple
448   Nehemiah rebuilds walls of Jerusalem
400   Intertestamental period begins
332   Alexander the Great conquers the Holy Land
330   Samaritans build their own temple
167   Maccabean revolt
164   Rededication of the temple
63   Roman General Pompey captures Jerusalem
37   Herod the Great rules Judea
7   John the Baptist born
5   Jesus of Nazareth born
4   King Herod dies

AD (CE)
26–36   Pontius Pilate governs Judea; Herod Antipas governs Galilee
28   Jesus begins his ministry
30   Jesus' crucifixion and resurrection
35   Conversion of Saul of Tarsus (Paul)
47   Paul begins missionary journeys
50–62   Paul's epistles to the churches written
65   Christians persecuted in Rome; Peter and Paul executed
66   Jewish revolt against Rome
70   Romans destroy the temple in Jerusalem
70–95   Gospels and Acts of the Apostles written

Chronology, Historical (approximate dating)

Stone Age (570 million years ago to 3000 BC)
    Early Stone Age (Palaeolithic)

Middle Stone Age (Mesolithic)
New Stone Age (Neolithic)
Early Civilization (5000 BC+)
Bronze Age (3000–1200 BC)
Iron Age (1200–500 BC)
Persian Period (500–323 BC)
Hellenistic Period (323–37 BC)
Roman Period (37 BC–AD 324)
Byzantine Period (324–640)
Middle Ages (500–1450)
Renaissance (1450–1750)
Age of Exploration (1490–1911)
Reformation (1500–1600)
Age of Colonization and Inventions (1600–1700)
Age of Revolution and Independence (1700–1815)
Industrial Revolution (1750–1900)
World Wars (1900–1946)
Cold War (1947–1991)
Information Age (1991–present)

English Bible Translations Timeline

1382 Wycliffe Bible
1525 Tyndale Bible (NT and Pentateuch)
1535 Coverdale Bible
1537 Matthew's Bible
1539 Archbishop Cramner's Great Bible
1560 Geneva Bible
1568 Bishop's Bible
1582 Douay Bible
1609 Roman Catholic Authorized Bible
1611 King James Version
1881 Revised Version
1901 American Standard Version
1946 Revised Standard Version
1961 New English Bible
1963 New American Standard Bible

1966   Jerusalem Bible
1966   Good News Bible (Today's English Version)
1970   New American Bible
1971   Living Bible
1978   New International Version
1982   Revised King James Version
1982   Reader's Digest Bible
1989   New Revised Standard Version
1989   New Revised King James Version
1994   Contemporary English Version

Four Horsemen of the Apocalypse (Revelation 6:2-8)
War
Famine
Pestilence
Death

Gifts of the Holy Spirit (1 Corinthians 12:4-11)
1. The utterance of wisdom
2. The utterance of knowledge
3. Faith
4. Gifts of healing
5. The working of miracles
6. Prophecy
7. The ability to distinguish between the spirits
8. Speaking in different kinds of tongues
9. Interpretation of tongues

Jewish Calendar Months
Tishri (Sep/Oct)
Cheshvan (Heshvan)
Kislev
Teveth (Tebet)
Sherat (Shebat)
Adar

Veadar (the 13th month in years 3, 6, 8, 11, 14, 17 of a 19-year
     cycle)
Nisan
Iyar
Sivan
Tammuz
Av (Ab)
Elul (Aug/Sep)

Jewish Canon
Torah (Pentateuch)
Nevi'im (Prophets)
Ketuvim (Writings)

Jewish Holy Days, Feasts, Fasts, and Festivals
1. Rosh Hashana, Feast of Trumpets (New Year); 1st day of Tishri
2. Fast of Gedalya
3. Yom Kippur (Day of Atonement); 10th day of Tishri
4. Sukkot (Feast of Tabernacles); 15th day of Tishri
5. Shmini Atzeret (8th day of Sukkot)
6. Simhat Torah (9th day of Sukkot)
7. Chanukah (Feast of Lights); 25th day of Chislev (8 days)
8. Fast of the 10th of Tevet
9. Tu Bishevat (New Year of Trees)
10. Ta'anit Esther (Fast of Esther)
11. Purim; 14th or 15th of Adar
12. Passover; 14th day of Nisan
13. Lag Omer
14. Shavout (Pentecost); 50 days after Passover in Sivan
15. Fast of the 17th Day of Tammuz
16. Fast of the 9th Day of Av

Judaism, Branches and Groups
Biblical
Essenes: apocalyptic sect
Karaites: rejected rabbinic Oral Law

Pharisees: emphasized ritual purity
Rechabites: emphasized faithfulness and self-discipline
Sadducees: rejected resurrection and immortality of the soul
Samaritans: emphasized Moses as the only prophet and stressed the
    sanctity of Torah

Modern

Conservative Judaism: holds traditional beliefs and practices within
    contemporary culture
Hasidism: emphasizes strict observance of laws
Kabbalism: Jewish mysticism
Orthodox Judaism: observes traditional believes and ways of life
    (*halakhah*) according to Torah and Talmud
Reconstructionist Judaism: emphasizes a left-wing rationalism
Reform Judaism: emphasizes moral and ethical teachings
Zionism: movement for Jewish homeland in Israel

Measures & Equivalents, Biblical

Weight:

Beka = 1/5 oz.
Shekel = 2 bekas (2/5 oz.)
Mina = 50 shekels (1 1/4 lb.)
Talent = 60 minas (75 lbs.)
NT Pound = 7/10 lb.

Volume:

Log = 2/3 pint
Omer = 1/10 ephah (2/3 gal.)
Hin = 12 logs (1 gal.)
Ephah (or Bath) = 6 bins (6 gal.)
Homer (or Cor) = 10 ephahs (60 gal.)

Length:

Finger = 3/4 in.
Hand-breadth = 4 fingers (3 in.)
Span = 3 hand-breaths (9 in.)

Cubit = 2 spans (18 in.)
Fathom = 6 ft.
Stadia = 200 yd.
Mile = 9/10 mi.

Membership of Major Religions (approximate)
Islam (1,000,000,000)
Hinduism (750,000,000)
Buddhism (350,000,000)
Eastern Orthodox (170,000,000)
Roman Catholicism (98,000,000)
Protestantism (45,000,000)
Sikhism (20,000,000)
Judaism (19,000,000)
Confucianism (6,000,000)
Bahai (5,000,000)
Shintoism (3,000,000)
Taoism (unknown)

Monetary Equivalents, Biblical
Denarius = one day's wages
Silver shekel = 4 denarii
Gold shekel = 15 silver shekels
Gold mina = 50 gold shekels
Gold talent = 60 gold minas
NT penny = 1/16 denarius

New Testament Books Chronology
Favoring an Early Dating:
AD 44–49	James
50–55	Mark
52	1 Thessalonians
53	2 Thessalonians
57	1 & 2 Corinthians
58	Galatians, Romans
58–60	Luke

60–66	Matthew
62–63	Ephesians, Colossians, Philemon
63	Philippians
63–64	Acts
64–65	1 Peter
65–68	Jude
65–66	1 Timothy, Titus
67	2 Timothy
66	2 Peter
67–68	Hebrews
90–95	John; 1, 2, 3 John
95–98	Revelation

Favoring a Late Dating:

AD 50/51	1 Thessalonians
51/52	2 Thessalonians
54–55	Galatians
56/57	1 Corinthians; 2 Corinthians
57/58	Romans
58–60	Philippians
58–60	Philemon
58–60	Colossians
65–68/70	Gospel of Mark
80s	Hebrews
80s–90s	James
85–90	Gospel of Matthew
Early 90s	Luke-Acts
circa 90	Ephesians
circa 90	1 Peter
90–100	Jude
90–100	Pastoral Epistles
90–110	Gospel of John; 1, 2, 3, John
95–96	Revelation
130 or after	2 Peter

Political Dynasties in the Intertestamental Era

Alexander the Great (336–323 BC)
The Ptolemies (323–30 BC)
The Seleucids (199–167 BC)
The Maccabees (167–134 BC)
The Hasmoneans (134–63 BC)
The Romans (63 BC–AD 135)
The Herodians (37 BC–AD 94)

Prophets and Their Ministry

Pre-Exile:
To Israel
   Hosea
   Amos
To Judah
   Habakkuk
   Isaiah
   Jeremiah
   Joel
   Micah
   Zephaniah
To Nineveh
   Jonah
   Nahum
To Edom
   Obadiah

Exile:
Ezekiel
Daniel

Post-Exile:
Haggai
Zechariah
Malachi
Author of Lamentations

Roman Emperors of the New Testament Era

Augustus (30 BC–AD 14)
Tiberius (AD 14–37)
Caligula (AD 37–41)
Claudius I (AD 41–54)
Nero (AD 54–68)
Galba (AD 68–69)
Otho (AD 69)
Vitellius (AD 69)
Vespasian (AD 69–79)
Titus (AD 79–81)
Domitian (AD 81–96)
Nerva (AD 96–98)
Trajan (AD 98–117)
Hadrian (AD 117–138)

Seder, Questions Asked at

1. Why is this night different from all other nights?
2. On all other nights, we eat all kinds of herbs; why on this night do we eat only bitter herbs?
3. On all other nights, we do not dip our food into condiments at all; why on this night do we dip it twice?
4. On all other nights, we eat sitting upright; why on this night do we recline?

Seven Last Words from the Cross (NRSV)

1. "Father, forgive them; for they do not know what they are doing." (Luke 23:34)
2. "Truly I tell you, today you will be with me in Paradise." (Luke 23:43)
3. "Woman, here is your son. . . . Here is your mother." (John 19:26-27)
4. "My God, my God, why have you forsaken me?" (Matt 27:46)
5. "I am thirsty." (John 19:28)
6. "It is finished." (John 19:30)
7. "Father, into your hands I commend my spirit." (Luke 23:46)

Stations of the Cross

1. Pilate's condemnation, Jesus sentenced
2. Jesus receives the cross
3. Jesus falls to the ground for the first time
4. Jesus meets his mother on the way
5. Simon of Cyrene takes the cross
6. Veronica wipes Jesus' face
7. Jesus falls for the second time
8. Jesus tells the women of Jerusalem not to weep
9. Jesus falls for the third time
10. Jesus is stripped of his clothing
11. Jesus is nailed to the cross
12. Jesus dies on the cross
13. Jesus' body is taken down from the cross and placed in Mary's arms
14. Jesus' body is entombed

Ten Commandments

1. You shall have no other gods before me.
2. You shall not make for yourself an idol.
3. You shall not make wrongful use of the name of the LORD your God.
4. Remember the sabbath day, and keep it holy.
5. Honor your father and your mother.
6. You shall not murder.
7. You shall not commit adultery.
8. You shall not steal.
9. You shall not bear false witness against your neighbor.
10. You shall not covet . . . anything that belongs to your neighbor.

Ten Plagues of Egypt

1. blood
2. frogs
3. gnats
4. flies
5. murrain (death of cattle)
6. boils

7. hail
8. locusts
9. darkness
10. slaying of the firstborn of Egypt

Three Temples of Jerusalem

First Temple: "Solomon's Temple" (c. 957–587 BC)
Second Temple: "Zerubbabel's Temple" (520–20 BC)
Third Temple: "Herod's Temple" (20 BC–AD 70)

Twelve Disciples

1. Peter
2. Andrew
3. James
4. John
5. Philip
6. Bartholomew
7. Thomas
8. Matthew
9. James
10. Thaddaeus
11. Simon
12. Judas Iscariot

Twelve Tribes of Israel

1. Reuben
2. Simeon
3. Judah (Levi)
4. Issachar
5. Zebulun
6. Dan
7. Napthali
8. Gad
9. Asher
10. Benjamin
11. Manasseh
12. Ephraim

Books, Journals, and Resources

Bible Versions, Best-Selling
1. New International Version
2. King James Version
3. New King James Version
4. The New Living Translation (Tyndale)
5. The Message, *Eugene Peterson* (NavPress)
6. New Century Version (Word)
7. New International Readers Version (Zondervan)
8. The Amplified Bible (Zondervan)
9. Contemporary English Version (Nelson)
10. The Living Bible, *Ken Taylor* (Tyndale)
[Source: Christian Booksellers Association]

Books Every Christian Educator Should Own
Thomas à Kempis. *Of The Imitation of Christ* (various publishers)
Augustine. *Confessions* (various publishers)
Dietreich Bonhoeffer. *The Cost of Discipleship* (Simon & Schuster)
Findley Edge. *A Quest for the Vitality of Religion* (Smyth & Helwys, 1994)
———. *Teaching for Results* (Broadman & Holman, 1995)
———. *The Greening of the Church* (Word Books, 1971)
Charles R. Foster. *Educating Congregations* (Abingdon, 1994)
Richard J. Foster. *Celebration of Discipline* (Harper & Row, 1988)
James Fowler. *Becoming Adult, Becoming Christian* (Harper Collins, 1984)
Edwin H. Friedman. *Generation to Generation* (Guilford Press, 1985)
Israel Galindo. *The Craft of Christian Teaching* (Judson Press, 1998)

Thomas H. Groome. *Christian Religious Education* (Harper & Row, 1980)

Edward Hammett. *Making the Church Work* (Smyth & Helwys, 1999)

Maria Harris. *Fashion Me a People* (Westminster/John Knox, 1989)

E. Glenn Hinson. *A Serious Call to a Contemplative Lifestyle* (Smyth & Helwys, 1993)

Morton Kelsey. *Can Christians Be Educated?* (Religious Education Press, 1977)

Malcolm S. Knowles. *The Modern Practice of Adult Education* (Association Press, 1970)

James M. Lee, ed. *The Spirituality of the Religious Educator* (Religious Education Press, 1985)

James M. Lee. *The Flow of Religious Instruction* (Religious Education Press, 1973)

Timothy A. Lines. *Functional Images of the Religious Educator* (Religious Education Press, 1992)

Leon McKenzie and Michael Harton. *The Religious Education of Adults* (Smyth & Helwys, 2002)

Gabriel Moran. *Showing How: The Act of Teaching* (Trinity Press, 1997)

Anthony Mottola, trans. *The Spiritual Exercises of St. Ignatius* (Image Book, 1964)

Henry Nouwen. *In the Name of Jesus* (Crossroad, 1989)

Richard R. Osmer. *Teaching for Faith* (Westminster/John Knox, 1992)

Parker J. Palmer. *The Courage to Teach* (Jossey-Bass, 1998)

Eugene C. Roehlkepartain. *The Teaching Church* (Abindon Press, 1993)

Lewis J. Sherrill. *The Struggle of the Soul* (Macmillan, 1951)

James D. Smart. *The Teaching Ministry of the Church* (Westminster Press, 1954)

Karen B. Tye. *Basics of Christian Education* (Chalice Press, 2000)

John H. Westerhoff III and John D. Eusden. *The Spiritual Life: Learning East and West* (Seabury Press, 1982)

James W. White. *Intergenerational Religious Education* (Religious
    Education Press, 1988)

Christian Publishers
Books
Abingdon Press (www.abingdon.org)
Augsburg Press (www.augsburg.com)
Augsburg Fortress Press (www.augsburgfortress.org)
Baker Book House (www.bakerbooks.com)
Barclay Press (www.barclaypress.com)
Beacon Hill Press (www.nazarene.org/co/beacon.html)
Bethany House Publishers (www.gospelcom.net)
Broadman & Homan (www.broadmanholman.com)
Cambridge University Press (www.cup.org)
Catholic University of America Press (www.cup.edu)
Chalice Press (chalicebks@aol.com)
Chariot Victor Books (www.chariotvictor.com)
Christian Publications (www.cpi-horizon.com)
College Press (www.collegepress.com)
Concordia Publishing House (www.cph.org)
Crossway Books (goodnewz@aol.com)
Faith & Life Press (flp@gcmc.org)
Gospel Light (www.gospellight.com)
Grace Publications (www.graceonline.com)
Group Publishing, Inc. (www.grouppublishing.com)
Harper San Francisco (www.harpercollins.com)
Harvest House (www.harvesthousepubl.com)
ICS Publications (www.ocd.or.at/ics)
Ignatius Press (www.ignatius.com)
Intervarsity Press (www.ivpress.com)
Judson Press (www.judson.com)
Kregel Publications (www.kregel.com)
Loyola Press (www.loyolapress.com)
Moody Press (www.moody.edu)
Navpress (www.navpress.org)
Oxford University Press (www.oup-usa.org)

Paulist Press (www.paulistpress.com)
Pilgrim Press (www.pilgrimpress.com)
Religious Education Press (releduc@ix.netcom.com)
Revell (Fleming H.) (www.bakerbooks.com)
Sheed & Ward (www.catalogmall.com/sheedw/index.tam)
Smyth & Helwys Publishing (www.helwys.com)
Tyndale House Publishers (www.tyndale.com)
Upper Room Books (www.upperroom.org)
Westminster John Knox Press (www.pcusa.org/ppc)
Zondervan Publishing House (www.zondervan.com)

Curriculum
Abbey Press (www.saintmeinrad.edu/abbeypress)
Abingdon Press (www.abol.com/login.htm)
Astrolabe Pictures, Islamic media outlet (www.astrolabepictures.com)
St. Anthony Messenger (www.americancatholic.org/index.html
Augsburg/Fortress Press (www.augsburgfortress.org)
Ave Maria Books (www.harb.net/AveMaria/index.htm)
Baptist Press (www.baptistpress.org)
Benzinger Press (www.benzinger.com/index.htm)
Catechist Magazine (www.catechist.com)
Channing-Bete Publishing (www.channing-bete.com)
Christian Book Distributors (www.chrbook.com)
Claretian Publications (www.claretianpubs.org)
Cokesbury Books (www.cokesbury.com)
Concordia Publishing (www.cphnet.org)
Creative Communications (www.grace-online.com/
    ministries/CreatComm/ccm.htm)
Youth Magazine, The United Methodist Church
    (www.gbod.org/youth)
Gateway Films/Vision Videos (www.catholicvideo.com)
Focus on the Family (www.family.org)
Grace Publications (www.ggwo.org/gracepublications)
Group Publishing (www.grouppublishing.com)
Guideposts (www.guideposts.org/gp2/index.shtml)

Harcourt Religion Publisher (134.11.73.2/religiousED/www.
   harcourtreligion.com)
Harold Shaw Publishers (www.shawpub.com)
Ignatius Press (www.ignatius.com/index.cfm)
Kerygma (kerygma.net)
Jewish Material (www.mesora.org)
Judson Press (www.judsonpress.com)
LifeWay Christian Resources of the Southern Baptist Convention
   (www.lifeway.com)
Liguori Press (www.catholic.org/liguori)
Liturgical Press (www2.csbsju.edu/litpress)
Logos (www.joinhands.com)
Moody Press (www.moody.edu/MP)
Navpress (www.gospelcom.net/navs/NP/store/welcome.html)
National Conference of Catechetical Leaders (www.nccl.org)
One Way Street, Inc. (www.onewaystreet.com)
Oregon Catholic Press (www.ocp.org)
Our Sunday Visitor (www.catholic.net/rcc/Periodicals)
Paulist Press (www.reliablehost.com/catholicshopper/page32.html)
Pflaum/Hi Time (www.pflaum.com)
The Printery House (www.msc.net/cabbey/printery/printery.html)
Resource Publications, Inc. (www.rpinet.com/index.html)
Resources for Christian Living (www.heraldoftruth.org/
   personal/resources/resources01.html)
St. Mary's Press (www.smp.org)
S&S Worldwide (www.criterioninfo.net/
   champions/roger/s&s_vivo_high.html)
Silver Burdett & Ginn (www.sbgschool.com)
Smyth & Helwys Publishing (www.helwys.com)
The Upper Room (www.upperroom.org)
US Catholic Conference Publishing Services
   (www.nccbuscc.org/opps)
Thomas Nelson Publishing (www.thomasnelson.com)
WordAction Publishing (www.nphdirect.com)
Zondervan Press (www.zondervan.com)

Journals and Periodicals for the Christian Educator

Arts: The Arts in Religious and Theological Studies

American Visions: The Magazine of African-American Culture

The American Journal of Family Therapy (www.taylorandfrancis.com)

Adult Education Quarterly (adultedquarterly@cornell.edu)

Adult Learning (202.429.5131)

Child Development (www.srcd_org/cdv/default.htm)

Childhood Education (www.acei.org)

The Christian Century (www.christiancentury.org)

Church Educator

Books & Culture: A Christian Review (www.booksandculture.com)

Christian Century (www.christiancentury.org)

Church History (www.churchhistory.org/journal)

Curriculum Journal (www.tandf.co.uk/ journals/routledge/
    0958546.html)

Family Ministry: Empowering Through Faith (www.fmef.org)

First Things (www.firstthings.com)

The Journal of Biblical Storytelling (513.791.2899)

Journal of Curriculum & Supervision (800-933-ASCD)

Journal of Developmental Education (www.ncde.appstate.edu)

Journal of Education and Christian Belief (www.atla.com)

Journal of Education for Teaching (www.tandf.co.uk/journals/
    carfax/02607476.html)

Journal of Education Psychology

The Journal of Experiential Education (www.aee.org)

The Journal of Moral Education (www.tandf.co.uk)

Journal of Philosophy of Education (www.blackwellpublishers.co.uk)

Journal of Religious Education

Journal of Ritual Studies (www.pitt.edu/~strather/journal.htm)

Journal of Research of Christian Education (jrce@andrews.edu)

Leadership: A practical journal for church leadership
    (www.leadershipjournal.net)

Ministries Today (www.ministriestoday.com)

Netresults (www.netresults.org)

Oxford Review of Education (www.tandf.co.uk/journals)

Religion and the Arts (cs@blillusa.com)

Religion Teacher's Journal (800-321-0411)

Religious Education (www.taylorandfrancis.com)

Review & Expositor: A consortium Baptist theological journal (502-327-8347)

Spiritual Life: A journal of contemporary spirituality (www.spiritual-life.org)

Strategies for Today's Leader (www.strategiesfortoday.org)

Studies in Spirituality (www.kun.nl/tbi/sis.html)

Teachers College Record (www.tcrecord.org)

Teachers and Teaching: Theory and Practice (www.tandf.co.uk/journals/carfax/13540602.html)

Teaching Theology and Religion (www.wabashcenter.wabash.edu)

Your Church (www.yourchurch.com).

Questions for Evaluating Curriculum Resources

1. Is there a clearly delineated set of learning objectives or aims?
2. Are the objectives biblical?
3. Are the objectives appropriate to congregational Christian education?
4. Do the objectives address both individual and corporate spiritual concerns?
5. Do the lessons call for appropriate, clear, and specific learner responses?
6. Does the overall scope of the Bible content reflect a balance between the Old and New Testaments?
7. Does the lesson connect Bible content with learners' life experiences?
8. Is the literature age-appropriate in content, themes, reading level, and teaching methods?
9. Does the literature reflect attention to sound theories of teaching and learning?
10. Does the literature reflect attention to sound theories of human personal development?
11. Is the role of the teacher clearly identified?
12. Are there helpful and practical teacher preparation support materials?

13. Are there attractive and helpful learner support materials?
14. Does the literature provide flexibility and options in teaching approaches and methods?
15. Is there provision for learning assessment in the lesson?
16. Are suggested activities and lessons consistent with learning outcomes?
17. Does the publisher provide a clear scope and sequence of lessons, themes, and biblical content?
18. Is there a balanced approach to addressing learners' intellectual and emotional, personal and social spiritual needs?
19. Is the literature appropriate or supportive of your church's denominational and doctrinal identity?
20. Is the material attractive, easy to comprehend, and intuitive in its layout?
21. If important to your church, is there attention to ethnicity, ecumenism, and gender-inclusive language?
22. Is the product reasonably priced?
23. Does the publisher provide online support for teachers, pupils, and churches?

Educational Foundations

Curriculum Development, Models of
1. Dick and Carey Design Model: systems approach
2. Gerlach-Ely Design Model: prescriptive model
3. Hannafin and Peck Design Model: three-phase, formative evaluation model
4. Jerrold Kemp Design Model: holistic approach to instructional design
5. Kirkpatrick's Design Model: hierarchical approach emphasizing evaluation and training
6. Knirk and Gustafson Design Model: three-stage process model
7. Tripp and Bichelmeyer's Rapid Prototyping Model: four-level process utilizing heuristics, experience, and intuition

Influential Educational Theorists
Socrates (470–399 BC)
Plato (427–347 BC)
Aristotle (384–322 BC)
Quintilian (AD 35–95)
Clement of Alexandria (150–c. 215)
Origen (185–254)
Augustine of Hippo (354–430)
Columba (521–597)
St. Benedict (628–689)
Alcium (735–804)
Thomas Aquinas (1225–1274)
Gerhard Groot (1340–1384)
Desiderius Erasmus (1466–1536)

Martin Luther (1483–1546)
Ignatius of Loyola (1491–1556)
Juan Luis Vives (1492–1540)
John Calvin (1509–1564)
John Amos Comenius (1592–1672)
August Hermann Francke (1663–1727)
John Wesley (1703–1791)
Robert Raikes (1735–1811)
Thomas Jefferson (1743–1826)
Johann H. Pestalozzi (1747–1827)
Thomas Arnold (1795–1841)
John Henry Newman (1801–1890)
Horace Bushnell (1802–1876)
John Dewey (1859–1952)
Maria Montessori (1870–1952)
Paulo Freire (1921–1997)

Influential Twentieth-century Christian Educators

Dorothy Bass
Harold W. Burgess
George Albert Coe
Gaines Dobbins
Craig Dykstra
Findley B. Edge
Howard Grimes
Thomas Groome
Maria Harris
James Michael Lee
Sara Little
James Loder
Randolph Crump Miller
Gabriel Moran
C. Ellis Nelson
Parker Palmer
John Milburn Price
Lewis Sherrill

James D. Smart
Elmer Towns
John H. Westerhoff III
D. Campbell Wyckoff

Philosophical Influences on Christian Education

Behaviorism (Watson)–Theory of human behavior that states that
actions can be explained entirely as responses to stimuli.

Empiricism (Locke)–Any theory that emphasizes sense-experience
rather than reason or intuition as the basis for knowledge.

Existentialism (Kierkegaard)–Distinguishes between the kind of *being*
possessed by humans from that possessed by objects. People as
being are essentially open-ended, free from determination from
pre-existing essence ("existence precedes essence"). Emphasizes
personal freedom, choice, and responsibility.

Functionalism–Theories that define things in terms of what they do
or the function they play in their relationships and environment.
Tends to define things in terms of their cause and effect; defines
cognition in terms of its effect on behavior.

Idealism (Plato)–The school(s) of thought that states that reality
exists or depends intrinsically and causally on the mind.

Inductivism–Epistemological view that inference in accordance with
some version of the inductive principle is logically valid or at least
rationally legitimate.

Instrumentalism–Philosophical view that laws and theories are not
interpreted as truth or as objective, but as instruments for the for-
mulation of hypotheses. A theory, belief, or value is judged in
terms of its usefulness rather than its correctness or "truth."

Intuition–Any philosophical view claiming that some of our
knowledge is attained by a direct process independent of the
senses and not open to rational assessment.

Neo-Platonism (Plotinus, Hegel)–A concept that strives to reconcile
the teachings of Plato and Aristotle. Reality is hierarchically
ordered.

Postmodernism (Jancks, Foucault)–The concept that instead of single
sets of values, truth, or political loyalties there is a wide variety of

groups and classes, aims and ideologies, each with mutually valid claims to truth.

Pragmatism (Dewey)–Pragmatism holds that the meanings of concepts or propositions lay in their effect on our experiences, senses, emotions, and practices.

Rationalism–Relating to theories emphasizing reason or intuition as the basis for acquiring knowledge or as the basis for moral judgment.

Realism (Kant)–The view that abstract concepts have a real existence and can be understood empirically; the view that the physical world has a reality separate from the mind.

Philosophy, Branches of

Epistemology–theories of knowledge, truth, theory, methodology, evidence, and analysis

Metaphysics–theories of existence, essence, space and time, self, God, and ultimate cause

Logic–theories of argument and reasoning, validity, proof, definition

Aesthetics–theories of beauty, art, taste, standards, criticism

Analytic Philosophy–theories that rely on analysis as central to the philosophical method

Cosmology–the study of the origin and structure of the universe

Ethics–theories of good, right, responsibility, and morals

Principles of Development

Erik Erikson's Stages of Psychosocial Development

1. Trust vs. Basic Mistrust (infancy). Virtue: Hope
2. Autonomy vs. Shame and Doubt (early childhood). Virtue: Will
3. Initiative vs. Guilt (early schooling years). Virtue: Purpose
4. Industry vs. Inferiority (schooling years). Virtue: Competence
5. Identity vs. Role Diffusion (adolescence). Virtue: Fidelity
6. Intimacy vs. Isolation (young adulthood). Virtue: Love
7. Generativity vs. Stagnation (adulthood). Virtue: Care
8. Ego Integrity vs. Despair (senescence). Virtue: Wisdom

James Fowler's Stages of Faith Development
1. Undifferentiated Faith (infancy)
2. Intuitive-Projective Faith (early childhood)
3. Mythic-Literal Faith (school years)
4. Synthetic-Conventional Faith (adolescence)
5. Individuative-Reflective Faith (young adulthood)
6. Conjunctive Faith (mid-life and beyond)
7. Universalizing Faith (rare)

Sigmund Freud's Stages of Psychosexual Development
1. Oral Phase (birth-8 months)
2. Anal Phase (1-2 years)
3. Phallic Phase (2-6 years)
4. Latency Phase (6-11 years)
5. Genital Phase (11-18 years)

Robert J. Havighurst's Developmental Tasks for Adolescents
1. Adjust to a new physical sense of self.
2. Adjust to new intellectual abilities.
3. Adjust to increased cognitive demands at school.
4. Develop expanded verbal skills.
5. Develop a personal sense of identity.
6. Establish adult vocational goals.
7. Establish emotional and psychological independence from parents.
8. Develop stable and productive peer relationships.
9. Learn to manage sexuality.
10. Adopt a personal value system.
11. Develop increased impulse control and behavioral maturity.

Robert J. Havighurst's Developmental Tasks for Adulthood
Early Adulthood (18-29)
1. Selecting a mate
2. Learning to live with a marriage partner
3. Starting a family
4. Rearing children
5. Managing a home

6. Getting started in an occupation
7. Taking on civic responsibility
8. Finding a congenial social group

Middle Age (30-59)

1. Assisting teenagers to become responsible, happy adults
2. Achieving adult civic and social responsibility
3. Reaching and maintaining satisfactory occupational performance
4. Developing adult leisure-time activities
5. Relating to spouse as a person
6. Accepting and adjusting to physical changes in middle age
7. Adjusting to aging parents

Later Maturity (60+)

1. Adjusting to decreasing physical strength and health
2. Adjusting to retirement and reduced income
3. Adjusting to death of spouse
4. Establishing affiliation with one's age group
5. Meeting social/civic obligations
6. Establishing satisfactory living arrangements

Malcolm Knowles's Dimensions of Maturity

FROM	TOWARD
1. Dependence	Autonomy
2. Passivity	Activity
3. Subjectivity (Me)	Objectivity (in reality)
4. Ignorance	Enlightenment
5. Small abilities	Large abilities
6. Few responsibilities	Many responsibilities
7. Narrow interests	Broad interests
8. Selfishness	Altruism
9. Self-rejection	Self-acceptance
10. Amorphous self-identity	Integrated self-identity
11. Focus on particulars	Focus on principles
12. Superficial concerns	Deep concerns
13. Imitation	Originality

14. Need for certainty Tolerance of ambiguity
15. Impulsiveness Rationality

Lawrence Kohlberg's Stages of Moral Development
Building on the work of Jean Piaget in cognitive development, Lawrence Kohlberg identified a progression of moral reasoning identified by developmental stages and progression.

Preconventional Level
  1. Punishment-and-obedience orientation
  2. Instrumental-relativist orientation
Conventional Level
  1. Interpersonal concordance or good boy/nice girl orientation
  2. Law and order orientation
Post-Conventional Level
  1. Social contract, legalistic orientation
  2. Universal-ethical-principle orientation

Abraham H. Maslow's Hierarchy of Needs
8. Transcendence (highest)
7. Self-actualization
6. Aesthetic
5. Knowledge and Understanding
4. Esteem
3. Belonging and Love
2. Safety
1. Physiological (lowest)

Jean Piaget's Stages of Cognitive Development
1. Sensorimotor Period (birth-2 years)
    First Stage (0-1 month): reflexive stage
    Second Stage (1-4 months): adaptive actions, primary circular reactions
    Third Stage (4-8 months): intentional acts, secondary circular reactions
    Fourth Stage (8-12 months): beginning of practical intelligence

Fifth Stage (12-18 months): active experimentation, tertiary circular reactions

Sixth Stage (18-24 months): mental inventiveness, early language development, reflective intelligence

2. Preoperational Thought Period (2-7 years)
First Period (2-4 years): egocentric language, perception dependent
Second Period (5-7 years): intuitive thinking plus perception

3. Concrete Operations Period (7-11 years)
Cognitive actions of inversion and reciprocity, de-centering of attention, cause and effect, logic

4. Formal Operations Period (11-15 years)
Not limited by perception, can imagine present, past, and future; intellectual framework complete

Lev Vigotsky's Theory of Speech Development

The soviet psychologist Vigotsky investigated the conscious thought processes of speech and thought. Progress in speech and thought are not parallel. Their two growth curves cross and recross. Vigotsky's four stages of speech development are:

1. Primitive or natural speech (birth-2 years)
   a. Sounds represent emotional release
   b. Sounds interpreted as social reactions
   c. Child says first words
2. Naïve Psychology (2-3 years)
   a. Words have symbolic function
   b. Grammatical structures used intuitively
3. Egocentric Speech (3-4 years)
   a. Running monologue related to activities
   b. Speech and thought interact to produce conceptual or verbal thought

4. Ingrowth Stage (7+ years)
   a. Child manipulates language in his or her head in soundless speech
   b. Logical memory and conceptual problem solving

Vigotsky's stages of conceptual thought development are:

1. Stage I—Thinking in Unorganized Congeries or Heaps
   Subphase I-A: Trial-and-error grouping
   Subphase I-B: Visual field organization
   Subphase I-C: Reformed heaps
2. Stage II: Thinking in Complexes
   Subphase II-A: Associative complexes
   Subphase II-B: Collection complexes
   Subphase II-C: Chain complexes
   Subphase II-D: Diffuse complexes
   Subphase II-E: Pseudoconcept complexes
3. Stage III: Thinking in Concepts

Principles of Learning
A. Newell's Soar Theory Principles
1. All learning arises from goal-directed activities; specific knowledge is acquired in order to satisfy goals (needs).
2. Learning occurs at a constant rate—the rate at which impasses occur while problem solving (average of 0.5 chunk/second).
3. Transfer occurs by identical elements and is highly specific. Transfer can be general if the productions are abstract.
4. Rehearsal helps learning provided it involves active processing (i.e., creation of chunks).
5. Chunking is the basis for the organization of memory.

B. F. Skinner's Operant Conditioning Principles
1. Behavior that is positively reinforced will reoccur; intermittent reinforcement is particularly effective.
2. Information should be presented in small amounts so that responses can be reinforced ("shaping").

3. Reinforcements will generalize across similar stimuli ("stimulus generalization"), producing secondary conditioning.

Carl Rogers's Experiential Learning Principles

1. Significant learning takes place when the subject matter is relevant to the personal interests of the student.
2. Learning that is threatening to the self (e.g., new attitudes or perspectives) are more easily assimilated when external threats are at a minimum.
3. Learning proceeds faster when the threat to the self is low.
4. Self-initiated learning is the most lasting and pervasive.

David Ausubel's Subsumtion Theory Principles

1. The most general ideas of a subject should be presented first and then progressively differentiated in terms of detail and specificity.
2. Instructional materials should attempt to integrate new material with previously presented information through comparisons and cross-referencing of new and old ideas.

Jean Piaget's Genetic Epistemology Principles

1. Children will provide different explanations of reality at different stages of cognitive development.
2. Cognitive development is facilitated by providing activities or situations that engage learners and require adaptation (i.e., assimilation and accommodation).
3. Learning materials and activities should involve the appropriate level of motor or mental operations for a child of given age. Avoid asking students to perform tasks that are beyond their current cognitive capabilities.
4. Use teaching methods that actively involve students and present challenges.

Jerome Bruner's Constructivist Theory Principles
1. Instruction must be concerned with the experiences and contexts that make the student willing and able to learn (readiness).
2. Instruction must be structured so that the student can easily grasp it (spiral organization).
3. Instruction should be designed to facilitate extrapolation and or fill in the gaps (going beyond the information given).

Lev Vigotsky's Social Development Theory Principles
1. Cognitive development is limited to a certain range at any given age.
2. Full cognitive development requires social interaction.

Patricia Cross's Adult Learning Theory Principles
1. Adult learning programs should capitalize on the experience of participants.
2. Adult learning programs should adapt to the aging limitations of the participants.
3. Adults should be challenged to move to increasingly advanced stages of personal development.
4. Adults should have as much choice as possible in the availability and organization of learning programs.

Robert Gagne's Conditions of Learning Principles
1. gaining attention (reception)
2. informing learners of the objective (expectancy)
3. stimulating recall of prior learning (retrieval)
4. presenting the stimulus (selective perception)
5. providing learning guidance (semantic encoding)
6. eliciting performance (responding)
7. providing feedback (reinforcement)
8. assessing performance (retrieval)
9. enhancing retention and transfer (generalization)

Principles of Teaching and Instruction

Benjamin S. Bloom's Taxonomy of the Affective Domain

The affective domain contains behaviors and objectives that relate to the person's emotional and values-forming domains. It encompasses likes and dislikes, attitudes, values, and beliefs.

1.0 Receiving (Attending)
    1.1 Awareness
    1.2 Willingness to Receive
    1.3 Controlled or Selected Attention
2.0 Responding
    2.1 Compliance in Responding
    2.2 Willingness to Respond
    2.3 Satisfaction in Response
3.0 Valuing
    3.1 Acceptance of a Value
    3.2 Preference for a Value
    3.3 Commitment
4.0 Organization
    4.1 Conceptualization of a Value
    4.2 Organization of a Value
5.0 Characterization by a Value or Value Complex
    5.1 Generalized Set
    5.2 Characterization

Benjamin S. Bloom's Taxonomy of the Cognitive Domain

The objectives classified as cognitive emphasize intellectual, learning, and problem-solving tasks. Oversimplified, the cognitive domain is concerned with knowledge.

1.0 Knowledge
    1.10 Knowledge of Specifics
    1.12 Knowledge of Specific Facts
2.0 Comprehension
    2.10 Translation
    2.20 Interpretation
    2.30 Extrapolation
3.0 Application

4.0 Analysis
 4.10 Analysis of Elements
 4.20 Analysis of Relationships
5.0 Synthesis
 5.10 Production of a Unique Communication
6.0 Evaluation
 6.10 Judgments in Terms of Internal Evidence
 6.20 Judgments in Terms of External Criteria

Timothy W. Brock's Development Process for Sunday School

1. *Know Thyself.* Develop an understanding of the nature and mission of our church and how the Sunday school ministry might help the church to achieve this mission.
2. *Create an Environment for Learning.* Create a learning congregation—a warm, caring, and thoughtful atmosphere where all can become disciples and mature in faith.
3. *Equip all Members for Service.* Assist each member (not just Sunday school leaders) to identify his or her ministry and gifts.
4. *Customize the Organization.* Create a variety of class options within each age group and offer optional Sunday school studies.
5. *Gather the People.* Offer educational and cultural experiences that address the changing needs of people in this community.

(Used with permission of Timothy W. Brock.)

Robert Gagne's Theory of Learning Tasks

Gagne's theory stipulates that there are several different types or levels of learning. The effective teacher understands that each different type requires different types of instruction. Gagne identifies five major categories of learning: verbal information, intellectual skills, cognitive strategies, motor skills, and attitudes. Different internal and external conditions are necessary for each type of learning. In addition, Gagne's theory outlines nine instructional events and corresponding cognitive processes:

1. gaining attention (reception)
2. informing learners of the objective (expectancy)
3. stimulating recall of prior learning (retrieval)
4. presenting the stimulus (selective perception)
5. providing learning guidance (semantic encoding)
6. eliciting performance (responding)
7. providing feedback (reinforcement)
8. assessing performance (retrieval)
9. enhancing retention and transfer (generalization)

Israel Galindo's Ten Theorems of Christian Education

1. Stick to the basics. If you don't know the basics, learn them.
2. Decide who you are before deciding what you'll do. Christian teaching flows out of who you are in relation to God and others, not from how well you can perform.
3. Process is more important than content.
4. No curriculum will solve your program problems. A good curriculum will provide structure, offer ideas, give biblical interpretation and cultural background information, and suggest a starting place for your teaching. A curriculum will not inspire you or your students, make you a better Christian, meet the particular needs of your learners, or solve your classroom problems. Curriculum is written for the widest possible audience. You're special. Your class is unique. Use curriculum to benefit your particular learners.
5. Good teachers facilitate learning; great teachers *inspire* learning.
6. People don't remember lessons; they remember relationships.
7. People learn in many ways, but each person has only five senses through which he or she learns. "Creativity and "innovation" only go so far before they become ineffective.
8. Learning never ends. It's a lifelong adventure.
9. There is no perfect program. There are good and better, valid and sound, and great and good enough. And any one of them is only good for its time because people grow and times change.
10. Learning is change. Teaching is not entertainment. Learning is not always fun. Change is difficult, sometimes painful, and often resisted. The kind of change (learning) we seek in Christian

teaching at its highest level is *metanoia*—"conversion." In the
final analysis, that's the work of the Spirit, and that's *real* change!

Howard Gardner's Multiple Intelligences

In his *Theory of Multiple Intelligences*, Howard Gardner proposes that
people are not simply "smart" or "dull." Rather, they have different
"intelligences." He has identified seven distinct multiple
intelligences:

- Verbal/Linguistic Intelligence
- Visual/Spatial Intelligence
- Musical Intelligence
- Logical/Mathematical Intelligence
- Bodily/Kinesthetic Intelligence
- Interpersonal Intelligence
- Intrapersonal Intelligence
- Naturalist Intelligence

Malcolm Knowles's Principles of Andragogy

In the field of adult education, andragogy is most closely associated
with the educator Malcom Knowles. For Knowles, andragogy is
premised on at least four crucial assumptions (the fifth listed below
was added later) about the characteristics of adult learners that differ
from the assumptions of pedagogy, which concerns itself with child
learners.

1. *Self-concept:* As a person matures, his or her self-concept moves
   from that of a dependent personality toward that of a self-directed
   human being.
2. *Experience:* As a person matures, he or she accumulates a growing
   reservoir of experience that becomes an increasing resource for
   learning.
3. *Readiness to learn:* As a person matures, his or her readiness to learn
   becomes oriented increasingly to the developmental tasks of social
   roles.

4. *Orientation to learning:* As a person matures, his or her time per-spective changes from one of postponed application of knowledge to immediacy of application, and accordingly his or her orienta-tion toward learning shifts from subject-centered to problem-centered.
5. *Motivation to learn:* As a person matures, the motivation to learn becomes internal.

David Kolb's Experiential Learning

Deeply rooted in the ideas of John Dewey, experiential learning is understood as a lifelong process in which learners are not passive, "empty vessels," but have personal needs, interests, experiences, and desires. Kolb's experiential learning is the process through which knowledge is created through experience. It includes four key concepts:

1. The emphasis is on the process of learning rather than content or outcome.
2. Knowledge is transformative, continuously created and re-created; it is not a set of dictums merely to be transmitted.
3. Learning changes a person's perspective about his or her new experiences.
4. The process of learning is tied to the notion of knowledge; to understand either requires understanding the other.

James McKenny's Four Learning Modes

1. PERCEPTIVE individuals bring to bear concepts to filter data. They focus on relationships between items and look for deviations from or conformities with their expectations. Their precepts act as cues for both gathering and cataloguing the data they encounter.
2. RECEPTIVE thinkers are more sensitive to the stimulus itself. They focus on detail rather than relationships and try to derive the attributes of the information from direct examination of it instead of by fitting it to their precepts.

3. SYSTEMATIC individuals tend to approach a problem by structuring it in terms of some method that, if followed through, leads to a likely solution.
4. INTUITIVE thinkers usually avoid committing themselves like the Systemic thinkers. Their strategy is one of solution testing and trial-and-error. They are much more willing to jump from one method to another, to discard information, and to be sensitive to cues that they may not be able to identify verbally.

Samuel Messick's Learning Styles
1. Field independence vs. field dependence
2. Scanning
3. Breath of categorizing
4. Conceptualizing style
5. Cognitive complexity vs. simplicity
6. Reflectiveness vs. impulsivity
7. Leveling vs. sharpening
8. Constricted vs. flexible control
9. Tolerance for incongruous or unrealistic experiences

Jack Seymour's Approaches to Christian Education
Jack Seymour identified what he called basic "approaches" to Christian education. Though somewhat modified in later publications, these early approaches provide a sound framework for encompassing Christian education.

1. Religious Instruction
2. Faith Community
3. Spiritual Development
4. Liberation
5. Interpretation

Personal Growth and Professional Survival

Breaking out of a Rut, Steps for

1. Take inventory of where you are in your life and vocation.
2. Take a walk somewhere you've never been.
3. Read poetry.
4. Count your blessings.
5. Play "What if…."
6. Take a mini-vacation.
7. Write your obituary.
8. Pray differently, or stop praying and just listen.
9. Shadow someone who works at something different from what you do.
10. Change your work environment.
11. Talk to your kids—they usually have a keen insight into what's going on.
12. Volunteer for a day at a preschool, nursing home, or hospice.

Burnout

Burnout is a professional hazard for clergy and church staff. Learning to recognize it in yourself and others is critical to personal growth and professional survival. The burnout cycle includes twelve phases:

1. Compulsion resulting from anxiety
2. Intensity, seriousness
3. Subtle personal deprivations
4. Denial of interpersonal conflict and personal needs
5. Distortion and collapse of personal values
6. Heightened denial

7. Disengagement from others and self
8. Discernible behavior and life pattern changes
9. Depersonalization
10. Feeling of emptiness
11. Depression
12. Total burnout characterized by exhaustion

Marty Canaday's "Ministry Tidbits"

• When making a presentation, use a 5.5-x-8.5 sheet of paper. This fits well in a Bible or small notebook and is easier to read than an 8.5-x-11 sheet. The smaller size is simple to format in your word processing program.

• Use short paragraphs when reading a sermon or presentation. Put all Scripture quotes in bold or italicized print. It helps break up paragraphs, making glancing at them easier.

• Carry a small notepad with you on Sundays and Wednesdays. Write down things people ask of you, or ask people to write down their requests for you. If you don't do this, you will often forget to follow through on promises. Always follow through on promises!

• Keep a toothbrush, toothpaste, hairbrush, mirror, pain reliever, and mints in your office at all times.

• Make it a regular habit to put the file name on every computer printout. This saves time trying to find a document you have saved.

• When singing from the pulpit stage, do not bury your head in the hymnal. Look out across the congregation as much as possible, singing from memory and glancing at phrases. Eye contact with your congregation is important.

• Don't be so serious all the time.

• Laugh at yourself when you make a mistake. Own up to your mistakes.

• Leave your office door open as much as possible. There is little more valuable to your ministry than to be perceived as approachable.

• Clean your office regularly. Professionals need not look like slobs!

• Send affirmation notes to parishioners on a regular basis.

- Choose your battles carefully. Some issues are not worth the risk of upsetting people.
- Be firm with expectations. Clearly present them, and then stick to them.
- Develop personal ministry goals whether your church asks you to do this or not. It will enhance your ministry.
- Make reading in your field a regular routine.

(Used by permission of Marty Canaday.)

Conflict, Ineffective Ways of Dealing with

1. Ignore it. (Face it directly.)
2. Avoid it. (Schedule a time to deal with it.)
3. Give in to it. (Don't placate or empower inappropriate sources of conflict.)
4. Hold to the belief that conflict is "bad." (It's part of life and if handled well can lead to health and growth.)
5. Try to win over your opponents by being nice. (Don't try to reason with unreasonable people.)
6. Win at any cost. (Winning is relative. You may win the battle and loose the war. Seek resolution, not victory.)
7. Take it personally. (Ninety-nine times out of a hundred, it's not about *you*.)
8. Keep it to yourself. (Share the pain; there's plenty to go around. Conflict belongs to all parties involved.)
9. Believe that once it's settled, it's "settled." (Conflict has a tendency to find a way to express itself. Recognize it when it comes around again.)
10. Transport it. (Keep your work conflicts at work and your home conflicts at home, and remember which is which.)

Dysfunctional Senior Pastor, Ways to Handle a

1. Pray for him or her.
2. Show loyalty as far as your conscience and principles allow.
3. Foster an honest and open working relationship.
4. Feed the neurosis and the over-function.

5. Do not take responsibility for his or her mistakes.
6. Do not make excuses for him or her.
7. Do not speak ill of the person in others' company.
8. Remember that the church called the pastor. Allow them the pain of their choice.
9. If you can no longer support the person or his or her ministry, seek another place to work out your calling.
10. Hold him or her accountable for actions, behavior, speech, and decisions only as these involve you and your ministry.
11. Guard your spirit.

Dysfunctional Staff Colleagues, Ways to Handle

• Pray for them.
• Pray for love and patience for yourself.
• Practice grace in trying to understand and accept the person.
• Express appreciation when they do something right (publicly and privately).
• Take them out to lunch and share your concerns honestly.
• Encourage them to grow professionally and personally.
• Be clear about your expectations for a personal and professional working relationship.
• Don't take responsibility for their mistakes; give them freedom to fail (and learn).
• Be frank with staff and supervising committees about actual and potential issues that threaten a professional working relationship.
• Treat them professionally and courteously.
• Do not speak ill of them in public.
• If you supervise them, hold them accountable to clear expectations and written guidelines (document incidents and performance-related conversations).
• If you supervise them, give yourself permission to let them go if it is within your authority; do not delay the process if the staff member shows no sign of being willing to change.

Enlistment, Steps for Effective

1. Identify ministry needs and pray for the best person for the job.
2. Identify best person for the job and meet with that person for a *formal* dialogue session.
3. Come prepared to the meeting: present job description, present resources, state expectations, explain support, tell why you think he or she is the best person for the ministry.
4. Answer questions but do not ask for a commitment at this time. Challenge the person to think and pray about the invitation.
5. Follow up with a visit or phone call for a decision.
6. If the answer is no, accept graciously.
7. If the answer is yes, invite the person to an orientation meeting.
8. Provide a formal orientation for the person:
   - Include a site visit (classroom or ministry location)
   - Introduce colleagues
   - Provide resources
   - Answer questions
   - Review job responsibilities, expectations, and support systems
   - Prepare them for success

Enneagram Types

The original Enneagram schema identifies the "types" only by number. Below are associative labels for ease of identification:

1. The "Type A" Perfectionist
2. The Helping Partner
3. The Industrious Achiever
4. The Empathizer
5. The Fringe Observer
6. The Insecure Inquisitor
7. The Manic Adventurer
8. The Controller
9. The Peacekeeping Diplomat

First Year on the Job, Things to Do on the

1. Get to know the people.
2. Contact the person who had your position previously—pick his or her brain.
3. Endear yourself to the church secretary.
4. Establish and announce your office hours.
5. Take your vacation . . . no matter what.
6. Learn to work the copier.
7. Learn to work with the janitor.
8. Find a support group and commit yourself to it.
9. Create a Tickler File.
10. Survey the last three years of committee meeting minutes and church newsletters.
11. Write a regular column in the church newsletter.
12. Attend as many committee meetings as you can.
13. Attend worship planning meetings and participate regularly in worship leadership.
14. Set and communicate short- and long-range ministry vision.

Functions of a Christian Educator

- Participating in the pastoral functions of the church as appropriate
- Shaping and articulating a vision for Christian education appropriate to context
- Teaching and interpreting the biblical story
- Supporting pastoral and church staff in their work
- Providing educational expertise to the church at large
- Supervising hired staff and volunteer educators
- Managing church and organizational resources
- Training church leaders and educators
- Designing and implementing church curriculum
- Programming for effective education, training, and nurture
- Providing resources for leaders, educators, and programs

Leaving a Place of Ministry

1. Practice prayer and discernment regarding your ministry.
2. Be honest about where you are in the process of leaving.

3. Never threaten to leave a ministry in reaction to crises.
4. When you decide to go, *go*—don't linger.
5. Inform the Senior Pastor first, then your colleagues, then a presiding church board or committee.
6. Submit your resignation in writing; be brief, courteous, and state your timetable for leaving.
7. Do not make recommendations about your position or the ministry unless asked.
8. Allow the people who care about you to say goodbye in the way they need to do so.
9. Inform local denominational staff of your move.
10. Make final corporate remarks or sermons positive and affirming.
11. Keep your negative opinions about "what's wrong" with the church to yourself. (You gave up the right to speak on those issues when you decided to leave.)
12. Settle all debts, close or transfer professional accounts, turn in all keys, and leave your vacated office spotless.

Listening, Characteristics of Effective

Effective listening is a complex skill to learn. Good listeners:

1. are genuinely interested in the person speaking and know how to encourage others to share about themselves.
2. take responsibility for their part of the conversation.
3. interpret words, tone of voice, body language, and cultural cues.
4. interpret what is being said both in content and emotion.
5. respond appropriately to what is being said.
6. determine the purpose of conversations: small talk, cathartic, informative, persuasive.
7. have the discipline not to talk about themselves before listening to others.

Meetings, Leading Effective

1. Be clear about and get consensus on the purpose of the meeting.
2. Provide an agenda and agree upon a dismissal time.

3. Let the participants know what is expected of them and help them be clear about their group roles.
4. Be prepared—information, helps, process tools.
5. Provide a comfortable and functional meeting environment.
6. Be proactive in determining the decision-making process of the meeting.
7. Provide fair and unbiased leadership.
8. Facilitate total involvement from all group members.
9. Deal with real issues openly and appropriately. Bring "hidden agendas" out into the open.
10. Seek, encourage, and respect different points of view.
11. Give participants responsibility for the meeting's success.
12. Engage the group in a mini-evaluation before dismissal.
13. Lead the group to assign follow-up responsibilities and action items with deadlines.

Meyers-Briggs Personality Types

The Meyers-Briggs Type Indicator (MBTI) is a psychological tool used to help people understand their personality preferences. The assessment is structured as a questionnaire that yields a four-letter personality "type." There are sixteen different types, each of which represents a unique combination of the four preferences: I–E (introvert–extrovert), N–S (intuitive–sensing), T–F (thinking–feeling), P–J (perceiving–judging):

INTP	INTJ	INFP	INSJ
ISTP	ISTJ	ISFP	ISFJ
ENTP	ENTJ	ENFP	ENFJ
ESTP	ESTJ	ESFP	ENFJ

Networking Strategies

1. Make good friends at college, graduate school, and seminary and stay in touch with them.
2. Send congratulatory notes, birthday cards, and Christmas letters.
3. Attend professional conferences and meetings.

4. Attend your denominational conferences, associations, and meetings.
5. Develop a keen interest in what others in your field are doing; ask them about it.
6. Let people know what you're up to—your accomplishments and the projects on which you work.
7. Get your name in print—write an article or a newsletter. Get elected.
8. Volunteer.
9. Identify people who maintain good networks and take them out to lunch. Don't talk business unless they ask.
10. Use the Internet, e-mail, and electronic media to make new contacts and expand your network.

Personal Growth for the Educator, Dimensions of

1. Practices of devotion and discipline in the spiritual life
2. Attention to physical wellness
3. Nurture of a healthy family life
4. Attention to professional development
5. Observance of a moral lifestyle
6. Attention to sound financial stewardship
7. Cultivation of sustaining relationships

Phrases You Should Never Use around Church Members

1. "That's not my job."
2. "I don't care."
3. "You know, your kid's a real brat!"
4. "Yes, I have a chauffeur's license."
5. "Yes, I know how to program the thermostat."
6. "Yes, my wife (husband) would be happy to play the piano for your program."
7. "Back off; I'm a professional; I went to seminary."
8. "I sure wish (*pastor, staff member*) would spend more time in the office."

Presentations, Tips for Creative

1. When presenting information, always use graphics (diagrams, cartoons, symbols, clip art, slides, overheads, etc.).
2. When giving a lecture or report, give an outline of your presentation and leave fill-in-the-blank sections for hearers to complete.
3. Present like a Bizarro (opposite and backward): present from the back of the room, start the meeting from the end of the agenda, or give the answers and ask listeners to tell you the questions.
4. Use a mind map to diagram your presentation as you talk.
5. Use music. Play music in the background, use it to call the group back from break, play a sing-along song to break monotony, examine lyrics, write a rap song, use a "theme song," etc.
6. Use focal points—physical objects that help convey the theme of your presentation, illustrate a concept, or symbolize an idea to which you can point throughout your presentation.
7. Use imaginative, colorful, central metaphors in explanations.
8. Use group process learning activities to help participants review, discuss, and manipulate complex ideas and concepts.
9. Incorporate elements that require various senses: smell, touch, taste, sound, sight.
10. Talk less and dialogue with participants more.
11. Always provide a handout or something your participants can take with them.
12. End your presentation early.

Support Groups, What to Look for in

- High level of mutual accountability from the group members
- Responsible leadership
- Clearly articulated purpose and expectations of membership
- Respectable group members
- Tolerance for honesty
- Commitment to meeting regularly
- High level of maturity among the members
- Good mix of veterans and newcomers
- Commitment to personal growth of the members

Work Habits, Effective

1. Maintain a to-do list.
2. Take a day off regularly.
3. Get to work early and leave on time.
4. Keep an uncluttered desk and office. (Regardless of what you may want to believe, it *does* reflect on you and your work.)
5. Don't read junk mail or junk e-mail.
6. Return calls during early morning or late afternoon.
7. Keep current in your professional reading.
8. Learn to delegate effectively.
9. Set realistic work goals and review periodically.
10. Remind yourself often of who you work for.
11. Maintain a strict line between the job of your ministry, your calling, and your home life.
12. Practice hands-on supervision for what you are responsible.
13. Learn to write efficient, concise memos. They help keep communication channels open and provide a record of work progress and decision-making.

Writing Advice

1. Keep a journal.
2. Write every day.
3. Publish a newsletter.
4. Read good literature.
5. Read books on writing.
6. Write letters.
7. Learn to type—even if it's using the hunt-and-peck method.
8. Have something to say when you write.
9. Write about what you know.
10. Avoid vagueness terms ("would," "may," "perhaps").
11. Be precise (say what you mean and mean what you say).
12. Write simply (leave the big words for the dissertation writing).
13. Prepare an outline before writing.
14. Edit your work, get someone else to edit it, then edit it again.
15. Put the work aside for two weeks, then review and edit it again.
16. Keep writing.

Programs

Children's Musicals (Popular)

Story-Tellin' Man by Ken Medema

Joseph and the Amazing Technicolor Dreamcoat by Andrew Lloyd Webber and Tim Rice (children's version)

Sam: The Story of the Good Samaritan by Bobby Hammack and Tom Adair

Oh, Jonah by Allen Pote and Carole McCann

Vivaldi's Gloria for Young Voices arr. by Tim Sharp and Vernon M. Whaley

I'm the Color of God by Walter Horseley

Elijah, Man of Fire (based on Mendelssohn's *Elijah*) by Austin Lovelace

The Tale of the Three Trees by Allen Pote and Tom S. Long

Angels, Lambs, Ladybugs and Fireflies by Betty Hager and Fred Bock

Rescue in the Night by Allen Pote and Tom S. Long

Church Programs, Effective

• Small-group Bible study
• Sunday school
• Women's Bible study and fellowship groups
• Men's Bible study and fellowship groups
• Drama groups
• Youth retreats
• Youth mission trips
• Clergy-church mentorship/internships
• In-depth Bible study groups
• Support groups (recover, divorce, parents, grief, job recovery, etc.)

- Vacation Bible School
- Intergenerational family retreats
- One-on-one discipleship mentoring
- Church picnics, dinners, banquets
- Group Spiritual Direction
- Short-term theme study (Lent, Advent, Bible book, life issue)
- Lay volunteer staff programs

Congregational Program Areas

A church's educational program will be shaped by several factors: history, denominational relations, size, location, predominant social class, identity, life stage, and leadership, for example. Below are essential congregational education program areas common to most churches:

1. Leadership Development
    - Continuing education for professional and paid staff
    - Calling out and development of lay leadership for organizational and program ministries
    - Calling out and development of future leadership
2. Pastoral Care Ministries
    - Ministries related to the spiritual care of individual congregational members
    - Ministries related to the spiritual care of the larger community
    - Ministries related to the spiritual care of families and their members
3. Educational Ministries
    - Engaging in discipleship of congregational members
    - Teaching the Bible, its content and meaning
    - Training the church educators and teachers
    - Providing spiritual growth opportunities and programs for church members and potential members
    - Providing resources for all church educational ministries
    - Planning, supervision, and administration of church educational programs

4. Music Ministries
- Engaging the congregation in participating in the spiritual dimensions of music
- Enhancing, leading, and educating the congregation in corporate and individual worship
- Providing spiritual growth opportunities and programs for church members and potential members through music

5. Outreach Ministries
- Reaching and teaching those outside of the church community
- Proclaiming the biblical message of Christ and the Church
- Providing the presence of Christ in the community and world

6. Missions Ministries
- Leading the congregation to engage in missions endeavors in the community and world
- Teaching and educating the congregation in denominational missions; its theology and practices
- Training congregational members and groups in missions endeavors
- Providing spiritual growth opportunities and programs for church members and potential members through missions endeavors

7. Congregational Development
- Working to ensure congregational health
- Leading the congregation in meaningful, authentic worship experiences
- Providing means for the congregation's organizational effectiveness
- Helping ensure sound and effective administration of the congregational resources
- Helping ensure the viability and relevance of the congregation as a local expression of the Body of Christ

Enlisting Workers and Teachers, Steps to

1. Prayerfully seek the best person for the job.
2. Make an appointment.

3. Describe the job and its expectations; explain support and resources available.
4. Challenge the person to consider the role prayerfully.
5. Allow time for the person to think and pray about it.
6. Follow up and ask for a decision.
7. Accept the person's decision.

New Programs, Steps to Developing

1. Assess the need and viability of the proposed program.
    a. Identify target group.
    b. Look for gaps in current programming.
    c. Look for gaps in participation by age or interest groups.
    d. Involve potential target audience in conversations and planning.
2. Determine appropriate educational and program approach.
    a. Choose best educational approach for program:
        Classroom (didactic)
        Experiential
        Small or large group
        Leader-dependent or group-directed
        Occasional or periodic
        Closed or open group or event
    b. Determine setting and space needs for program type and size of group.
3. Identify, recruit, and train leadership.
    a. Choose the best people for the job.
    b. Provide training and ongoing support.
    c. Provide budget and resources.
    d. Commit to ensuring the leadership's success.
4. Develop and launch the program.
    a. Promote program through general media.
    b. Promote program to target audience.
    c. Promote program through individual participant recruitment.
    d. Coordinate program with church calendar.

Retreats, Steps to Leading

1. Identify the type of retreat:
    - Contemplative or issue-oriented (grief, creativity, spirituality)
    - Group (parents, divorced, young adults)
    - Seasonal (winter, summer, Lent)
2. Choose a memorable theme.
3. Choose a site appropriate to the retreat purpose.
4. Identify your target audience and their needs and interests.
5. Be specific about what you want participants to get out of the experience.
6. Remember that a retreat is *not* a workshop.
7. Work with a collaborative group for planning; encourage creativity.
8. Determine and seek appropriate retreat leadership.
9. Schedule plenty of "free" time.
10. Plan an icebreaker for first session.
11. Provide "enhancements": refreshments, snacks and treats, disposable cameras, board games, writing materials, craft materials, sports equipment, appropriate music, theme-related skits, theme-related readings and videos.
12. Create an attractive, colorful brochure or flyer.
13. Announce the retreat four to five months before the event.
14. Limit attendance as appropriate for the nature of the retreat.
15. Plan to follow up with participants.

Teaching and Instruction

Attention

Ten Ways to Get Your Class's Attention

In order to move your class along, either in transition points in your lesson or just getting the learning session started, you need first to get their attention. In group settings it is important to get everyone's attention at the same time for instruction, directions, or sharing important information before moving on. Having everyone's attention helps avoid disruptions and discipline problems and keeps you from repeating yourself. Here are ten ways to get your group's attention:

1. *Shout.* But don't shout in desperation—that just means you've lost control. A "group shout" will get everyone focused and participating. If one or two learners did not participate, tell the class (not the individuals) that they didn't shout loud enough and have them try again. Obviously, you should use this method sparingly.

2. *Play music.* Play a rousing piece of marching music or a catchy rock-guitar riff on tape. Train your class that this is a signal to "stop and listen." You can also train your class to listen for quiet music as a signal to settle into a reading time or nap time.

3. *Clap in rhythm.* To get your class's attention, begin clapping in rhythm and signal for them to follow along. You can give instructions for the next step in your lesson by speaking in rhythm, "Put (clap) your (clap) papers (clap) down (clap) and (clap) place (clap) your (clap) chairs (clap) in (clap) a (clap) circle."

4. *Sing instructions.* This is effective with children, but can also get the attention of a group of adults having trouble moving on to the

next step in your lesson. You don't have to have a good singing voice to use this method; remember that your goal is to get their attention.

5. *Raise your hand.* This is effective especially if you train your group to raise their hands and pay attention. Using this method, you will not have to raise your voice and the group will help by getting the attention of anyone who hasn't raised their hand.

6. *Show an object.* Use an object as a point of focus and to signal that the class should pay attention to you. Your object can be a surprise you pull from under a table, a large sealed brown paper bag you place on the table to create intrigue, or an object your class is trained to respond to, like a "talking stick."

7. *Whisper.* As a rule, whispering is a more powerful attention-getter than raising your voice. Talk in a low voice as you give instructions or directions and watch how your class strains to pay attention.

8. *Play an instrument.* Even if you're not proficient at it, tooting on a wind instrument or playing a chord on a keyboard will get your class's attention. You might even sing or play a transitioning song. Once you get everyone's attention, move the group to the next step.

9. *Tap on shoulder.* Quietly tapping your learners on the shoulder and maintaining eye contact can get the attention of one or two learners without disrupting the rest of the class. Or you can go around and tap the entire class on the shoulder and have them follow you to the next learning station.

10. *Turn off the lights.* An old technique and a bit abrupt, sudden darkness still works. Turn off or flicker the lights in the classroom to get the class's attention, but give your directions immediately. As with all stimulus-response techniques, this one can lose its effectiveness if used too often.

Eight Ways to Sustain Attention
1. Use audio-visuals.
2. Move around when teaching.
3. Vary volume and pitch when speaking.
4. Use humor if appropriate to subject matter.

5. Guard against outside distractions.
6. Involve the student in the lesson.
7. Talk about topics of interest to your students.
8. Maintain eye contact with the listeners.

Attitudes and Values, Elements for Teaching

1. Write out and state the attitude to be learned as a learning objective.
2. Provide models for learners to observe and imitate.
3. Ensure a positive emotional experience and environment in the context for which the attitude change is intended.
4. Provide learners with accurate information about people, objects, or ideas toward which the change in attitude is sought.
5. Rely on group techniques and processes (role-play, peer pressure, group decision-making, etc.).
6. Provide for practice and expression of the learned attitude or value in its appropriate setting.

Body Language

1. To communicate which learner is to participate in an activity:
   - smile at the designated learner.
   - focus your eyes on the learner.
   - nod at the learner.
   - turn your body toward the learner.
   - point to the learner.
   - walk toward the learner.
   - touch the learner on the shoulder.
2. To communicate different messages to the learner:
   - use appropriate facial expression (frown, smile).
   - shrug your shoulder.
   - make an appropriate hand gesture (like the universal "okay" or "thumbs up" signs).
   - lean toward or away from learners to show interest, anticipation, or distancing .
3. To get your learners' attention:
   - walk to the front of the room

- stand at attention.
- survey the class or group and make eye contact.
- hold up your hand, tap a desk, flicker the lights, or ring a bell.
4. To deal with learner misbehavior:
  - turn your body toward and focus your eyes on the off-task learner.
  - frown at the learner.
  - raise your eyebrows.
  - wave your hand at the offending learner.
  - point your finger at the learner.
  - walk toward the misbehaving learner.
  - put your hand on the shoulder of the misbehaving learner.
  - put your hand on the desk of the inattentive learner.
  - sit near the learner.

Childhood ADD/ADHD, Typical Symptoms of

1. failing to give close attention to details or making careless mistakes
2. difficulty sustaining attention
3. appearing not to listen when spoken to directly
4. not following through on instructions and failing to complete tasks
5. organizational difficulties
6. avoiding or not liking tasks that require sustained mental effort
7. losing things necessary for tasks
8. easily distracted
9. forgetfulness
10. fidgeting
11. leaving their seat inappropriately
12. feelings of restlessness or excessive activity
13. difficulty engaging in leisure activities quietly
14. talking excessively
15. blurting out answers before questions have been completed
16. impatience, difficulty waiting
17. interrupting others in activities or conversation

Concepts and Generalizations, Steps for Teaching

1. Determine what level of mastery you want the learners to attain for the concept (see Bloom's Taxonomies, above).
2. Give the correct terminology for the concept you are trying to teach.
3. Give a definition of the concept.
4. Give learners opportunities to differentiate between examples and non-examples of the concept.
5. Help learners identify the "defining attributes" of the concept.
6. Give opportunity for learner feedback on the concept they are trying to learn.
7. Provide opportunities for the learners to apply the new concept in understanding principles and solving problems.

Critical Thinking

Ten Ways to Help Your Learners Develop Critical Thinking
Socrates said, "The unexamined life is not worth living." And so it is with faith: an unexamined faith is not worth much either. One of the most important characteristics of a mature faith is the ability to examine critically one's beliefs, values, assumptions, and religion.

Wilson Mizner said, "I respect faith; but doubt is what gets you an education." Here are ways to help your learners think critically about their faith:

1. *Ask learners to choose items from a list.* Choosing from a list of items forces the learner to create criteria for choosing. Follow up by asking the learner the rationale for their choice. Ask them to explain how they arrived at that rationale.
2. *Let the learner work a puzzle.* Puzzles are a good warm-up activity for critical thinking sessions. Invite the learners to explain how they went about solving the puzzle: intuition, logic, experience, inductive, or deductive reasoning.
3. *Have the learner match items in one list with items in another.* Matching items forces the learner to look for shared qualities, a basic component to understanding concepts that relate to the idea of a class of objects. And let's face it, faith necessitates

understanding some pretty heavy concepts: love, hope, faith, redemption, good, evil, eternity, salvation, etc.

4. *Direct the learner to carry out an experiment.* The process of carrying out an experiment calls upon the learner to use all the steps of the cognitive taxonomy: knowledge, comprehension, application, analysis, synthesis, and evaluation.

5. *Use thematic apperception dialogue.* In this method, a learner examines a picture of people interacting in a certain context and is asked to describe what is happening and what the people are thinking and feeling. Follow-up dialogue allows the learner to work on critical self-awareness of perception, assumptions, and prejudices.

6. *Ask the learner to judge the merit of an argument.* Judging forces the learner to form an idea, opinion, and estimate on the matter of hand. It calls on the learner to draw on previous knowledge and personal experience and to take seriously another person's point of view.

7. *Have the learner critique a poem, painting, film clip, book, or article.* Critiquing forces the learner to engage actively with ideas behind products (films, works of art, or literature), rather than accepting uncritically the messages and values behind those works.

8. *Instruct the learner to compare similar ideas, items, or arguments.* Comparing similar ideas forces the learner to identify the nuances between arguments and get behind the motivations for those arguments. This is especially useful in helping learners work at moral reasoning.

9. *Guide the learner to predict the outcome of a situation and share their reasoning.* Predicting an outcome causes learners to weigh determining factors, draw on experience, spot trends and patterns, and deal with factors imagined but yet unknown.

10. *Have the learner revise a story or article.* Revising stories or articles fosters the ability to think of alternatives to presented ideas. It allows the learner to develop counter arguments as they critically assess a point of view or conclusion.

Discussion

Five Ways to Prompt Good Class Discussion

Every good teacher knows that group members learn best when they participate. But getting learners to enter into a class discussion or to share their views is difficult. Here are five ways to help start a good discussion:

1. *Use a "talking stick."* A talking stick is an ancient dialogue technique used in many cultures. After a topic of discussion or a problem is presented to the group, the talking stick is passed around the circle from one person to the next. Whoever has the stick must speak to the issue at hand as everyone else listens. Once everyone has a turn, someone can ask for the talking stick to speak or respond. (Your talking stick can be anything from a wooden spoon to a craft stick.) For added fun, use a large stick with elaborate decorations.

2. *Agree-disagree cards.* Given a topic, write various opinions about the issue on 3-x-5 cards. You'll need at least three cards for each person. Shuffle the cards and distribute to the group. Instruct the group members to read each card, decide whether they agree or disagree with the statement, and why. Next, the members try to trade cards with which they disagree for cards with which they agree. They do this by telling the other person why they feel and think as they do. You can think of other variations on this activity.

3. *Case studies.* Case studies are great ways to get people talking. Write a brief case study about the topic under discussion. You can make it open-ended and controversial, but realistic. Give concrete information, and provide the group with one or two questions to address based on the situation. You might form several smaller groups, with each group taking a different point of view or answering a different set of questions. Debrief with the group afterward.

4. *Play "What if?"* Read a passage of Scripture or focus on the topic at hand and prompt your learners to come up with as many "What if?" questions as they can. Once you have compiled a list of their suggestions, choose one or two scenarios to explore.

5. *Play "But I'd Like Your Opinion."* For this technique, use an object similar to the Talking Stick. Instead of group members asking for the object, however, they give it to another person to hear their opinion. You can start by giving your opinion about the Bible passage, issue, or topic under discussion. When you've shared your thoughts, say, "But I'd like your opinion," and pass the object (talking stick, ball, wooden block, etc.) to another class member. That person must then share what he or she thinks or feels about the issue under discussion and then pass the object to another person, saying, "But I'd like your opinion." At the end of this activity, debrief the class on the opinions shared and continue with the discussion or with the next step in the lesson.

Effective Explanations, Methods for

1. Be clear about the purpose of the explanation before you begin.
2. Find a frame of reference for the learner and begin there.
3. Use an informal and conversational style.
4. When describing processes and procedures, strive for clarity and simplicity. Use lists or delineate steps.
5. Use visuals (graphs, charts, diagrams, illustrations).
6. Use vivid descriptions and emphasis.
7. Use analogies to help hearers grasp abstract ideas and processes.
8. Structure your explanation to focus on one idea, thought, or meaning at a time.

Factual Information, Methods for Teaching

1. Organize your material into no more than four or five "chunks" (main ideas) per learning session.
2. Help the learner make connections between what you are teaching and what they already know.
3. Organize more complex material into smaller, simpler components.
4. Present ideas and concepts in the precise form in which the learner needs to recall it.
5. Ensure that learners can give you a correct response the first time they are asked.

6. Provide ways for learners to use the new information in practical contexts immediately, then over the course of time.
7. Provide immediate feedback when assessing mastery and retention of new information.
8. Provide ways for learners to evaluate the accuracy and efficacy of the new information learned in groups and individually.

Groups

Best number of people in a group for discussion: 3
Best number of people in a group for case studies: 4-5
Best number of people in a group for problem solving: 9
Maximum number of people for an effective sharing group: 15

Learner Retention

Typical learners retain:

10% of what they hear
20% of what they read
50% of what they see
90% of what they do

Learner Retention Rates
1. Hearing only
      After three hours: 70% retention
      After three days: 10% retention
2. Seeing only
      After three hours: 72% retention
      After three days: 20% retention
3. Hearing and seeing
      After three hours: 85% retention
      After three days: 65% retention
4. Doing
      After three hours: 95% retention
      After three days: 90% retention

Music

Music is a part of the daily lives of most of our learners. It seems strange therefore that we do not incorporate it into our teaching more often. Music is one of the intelligences identified by educator Howard Gardner, and it has been shown to aid learning. Here are ten ways to use music in your teaching:

1. *Play a recording.* Enhance your teaching by playing a recording using a cassette tape or compact disc. You can use music as background noise for small group work. Highlight a particular song that relates to the lesson. Play contemporary popular songs and have your learners think critically about the content of the lyrics.
2. *Have a performance.* You've probably got hidden musical talent in your class. Encourage your learners to use their musical skills in the lesson. Explore ways talents and gifts relate. Highlight the value of the discipline of practicing for proficiency. Investigate ways music speaks to that person's spiritual life.
3. *Write a hymn.* Use the tune of a familiar hymn and have your class write new lyrics relating to the topic they are studying.
4. *Sing a song.* Begin your class with a rousing song. Or end your session with a quiet meditative song or familiar hymn.
5. *Tap out a rhythm.* Help your learners memorize a passage of Scripture by having them tap out the rhythm of the words. Repeat until they have learned the passage by heart.
6. *Play musical chairs.* Break up a long session by playing a game of musical chairs. Get the class pumped up and inject a little fun into the learning experience.
7. *Play a note code puzzle.* Teach your class members the letter names of notes (ABCDEFG) and have them create or solve a letter substitution puzzle.
8. *Create a band.* Provide rhythm instruments, harmonicas, kazoos, tambourines, etc., and lead the class in a performance to express celebration or as a way to teach cooperation. Form two groups and challenge them to make up lyrics as you go along.

9. *Circle dance.* Circle dances are simple to learn and provide a wonderful mix of music, text, and movement. Provide plenty of space, or if weather permits, perform outside.

10. *Contrast music styles.* Introduce your class to different ethnic music, religious and secular "spiritual" music, classical and contemporary music. Lead them to contrast the styles and explore ways they communicate, ways they elicit emotions, and ways some styles feel more familiar than others.

Physical and Manipulative Skills, Steps for Teaching

1. Assess the learners' current skill and developmental level related to what you want to teach.
2. Provide a demonstration of the skill to be learned.
3. Provide learners with verbal instructions for carrying out the sequence of actions involved in the skill.
4. Provide for practice of the skill.
5. As much as possible, make the conditions of practice as close to the actual conditions under which the skill will be used.
6. Make practice periods brief, over a length of time, with short intervals between practice sessions.
7. Provide immediate feedback correcting inadequate behavior and identifying and praising incremental skill mastery.

Praise

Characteristics of Effective Praise

Every teacher knows that giving praise to individual learners and to the class is important to fostering learning. But giving praise incorrectly or inappropriately can actually be detrimental to learning. The key is to give effective praise that:

- is contingent.
- identifies specific particulars of accomplishment.
- is spontaneous, varied, and credible.
- recognizes effort made toward success at difficult tasks.
- attributes success to effort and ability.
- fosters endogenous attributions.

- rewards attainment of specified performance criteria.
- presents information about competence.
- helps the learner appreciate task-related behavior.
- uses the learner's prior accomplishment as context.

Characteristics of Ineffective Praise
1. Delivered randomly or unsystematically
2. Restricted to global positive reactions
3. Bland and uniform
4. Rewards mere participation
5. Has no regard for the effort expended
6. Attributes success to ability alone or to external factors
7. Fosters exogenous attributions
8. Provides no information
9. Orients learners toward comparisons with others
10. Uses accomplishments of peers as context for others' performance

Ruining Your Lesson, Steps to
1. *Fail to pray and depend on your own strength.* Christian teaching is as much a spiritual discipline as any other path to spiritual growth. Praying is a given. Ask God for a clear mind, a creative spirit, and an open heart.
2. *Use the same methods week after week.* It's been said that the worst method is the one you use all the time. Vary your methods according to your lesson content and aim. Don't be afraid to experiment!
3. *Wait until the last minute before reading and preparing your lesson.* Preparing a good lesson is a process. The earlier you start, the more creative and insightful your teaching will become.
4. *Choose to lecture rather than lead discussions.* A surefire way of being labeled "boring" is to fill up the lesson time with the sound of your voice. Your learners will get more out of the lesson when you give them the opportunity to discuss, explore, question, and take part in the learning process.
5. *Be the expert; give the answers.* Effective teachers know how to use questions to help their learners discover the answers for

themselves. There are no experts in the Christian life; help learners learn how to ask the right questions for themselves.

6. *Don't attend teacher workshops or training opportunities.* It doesn't take long to become stagnant in ideas and skills. Make it a point to be a lifelong learner yourself. The best teachers are good learners.

7. *Show up late to class every time.* It won't take long for your learners to get the message: participating in formal Christian education is not important to you.

8. *Don't use audio-visuals.* Our culture has an ever-increasing dependence on icons, images, and graphics. Use information processing domains to which your learners are accustomed.

9. *Concentrate on the lesson and not on relationships.* People come together in Bible study more for personal needs than for intellectual needs. In the long run, your learners won't remember the lessons you've taught—they'll remember the relationship you nurtured with them.

10. *Wing it.* You can only get so much mileage out of "residual knowledge." And frankly, you just can't fool your learners for long. They'll perceive your lack of preparation as a statement of their worth in your eyes.

11. *Follow your teacher's guide to the letter.* Your teaching resource is a starting point, not an end. Whoever wrote the material doesn't know you or your class members. Adapt the material to fit your needs and the needs of your learners. Strive for relevance. If the lesson aim doesn't speak to you or to the needs of your class, change it! You are the teacher. You are called to teach.

Stages of Learning
Infants and Toddlers as Learners
• see themselves as the center of their world
• learn by sensory experience: tasting, feeling, touching
• need safety limits without lengthy explanations
• desire to avoid physical punishment leads to a need for approval of others and develops into cooperative behavior
• learn self-control as they test what is and what is not permissible

- perceive reliability, trust, and intuitive faith as others lovingly meet their basic needs
- parallel play is normal
- sharing is rare and difficult for toddlers
- imitation is an important vehicle for learning
- need to be allowed to make mistakes as part of the learning process of discovery

Preschoolers as Learners

- can learn through pictures and sounds connected with experience
- recognize themselves as part of an expanding world (family, others)
- language develops as does sense of self, which can be expressed in rebellion ("no")
- trust paves way for commitment to values accepted as "good"
- respond to positive affirmations and genuine praise
- can relate to God as love through parents and teachers
- can relate to active Bible stories
- can participate in rhythmic songs
- learn by doing and observation
- dreams are real to them/no distinction between living and non-living

Younger Elementary Children as Learners

- kindergartners increasingly manage their bodies and attend to group activities
- can find joy in their growing faith in relating to others in church
- understand obedience to a Heavenly Parent as they try to please adults
- susceptible to feelings of guilt unless discipline and guidance are free of shame
- feelings and action in Bible stories are powerful influences during this fantasy-filled stage
- need to use all their senses to discover Bible truths
- have difficulty recognizing concepts in a different form or context
- beginning to generalize concepts into larger patterns of knowing ("mom" is also "parent")

- tend to be literal and live in the here and now
- need to have their complaints taken seriously, but can be satisfied by a simple display of sympathy
- have a strong sense of "fairness"

Older Elementary Children as Learners
- strong reliance on rules leads to growing sense of justice and fairness
- concrete thinkers comfortable with "an eye-for-an-eye" theology
- may be uncomfortable with a God who is "out there" or who is "everywhere" or "within us"
- can accept "no one knows for sure" answers in matters of faith
- can handle 10-15-minute discussions tied to stories with concrete applications (crafts, games, memorization)
- can appreciate humor and some puns
- enjoy learning and handling the Bible

Teenagers as Learners
- cooperation with others is important after about age 11
- can begin to incorporate opposites in their lives
- can order their thoughts, work out hypothetical possibilities, and use logic
- limited by egocentrism—can fiercely hold on to ideas not tested in reality
- can participate significantly in group discussion
- can accept other viewpoints and weigh their merits
- reliance on external faith authority gives way to internal, reflective faith
- peer pressure can cause conformity of ideas and beliefs based on significant friends
- forming a strong identity and sense of self is paramount at this stage
- do not respond well to sermonizing, but can respond to challenges

Adults as Learners

- can continue to learn and grow as individuals through later stages of life
- need comfortable, non-threatening learning environment
- need to see immediate relevance and application of Bible learning to daily living
- may need to overcome internal and external obstacles to participation
- can respond to challenge if not embarrassed, threatened, or overwhelmed
- often have too many choices and options, so learning opportunities must be perceived as worth their time
- up to one-third of adults still operate on an adolescent thinking and feeling level

Teaching Methods

Art Teaching Methods

1. Block painting
2. Blow painting
3. Bulletin board
4. Cartoon/comic strips
5. Clay sculpting
6. Coat of arms
7. Collage
8. Crayon etchings
9. Crayon resist
10. Crayon rubbings
11. Diorama
12. Dough sculpture
13. Drawing
14. Exhibit
15. Finger painting
16. Frieze
17. Gadget painting
18. Illustration

19. Map
20. Melted crayons
21. Mobile
22. Montage
23. Mosaic
24. Mural
25. Paper tearing/cutting
26. Papier-mâché
27. Picture study
28. Poster
29. Puppet-making
30. Rebus
31. Sand painting
32. Spatter painting
33. Sponge painting
34. Stitching
35. String painting
36. Tempera painting
37. Thematic apperception

Critical Thinking Teaching Methods
1. Outlining
2. Graphing and extrapolating
3. Diagramming
4. Summarizing
5. Interpreting
6. Relating
7. Classifying
8. Researching
9. Evaluating
10. Identifying fact or opinion
11. Generalizing
12. Drawing parallels
13. Dialogue
14. Question and answer
15. Self-correcting

16. Applying criteria
17. Hypothesizing

Drama Teaching Methods
1. Acting out a Bible event
2. Choral speaking
3. Contemporary Bible skit
4. Dialogue
5. Discussion starter
6. Dramatic interviews
7. Monologue
8. Puppets
9. Pantomime
10. Radio and TV format
11. Role-playing

Music Teaching Methods
1. Group singing
2. Hymn reading
3. Hymn-text study
4. Lyric writing
5. Recordings

Paper and Pencil Teaching Methods
1. Charts
2. Creative Writing
    Dialogue
    Diary
    Journal
    Drawing
    Letters
    Monologue
    Newspaper articles
    Paraphrase
    Poetry: topic poem
    Poetry: free verse

3. Graph

4. Jot sheet

5. Map

6. Sentence response

7. Notebook

8. Puzzle

    Acrostic

    Coded message

    Crossword puzzle

9. Quizzes

    Definitions

    Fill in the blanks

    Multiple-choice

    Matching items

    Open-ended statements

    Pretest

    Posttest

    True-false statements

10. Time line

11. Unsigned written responses

12. Worksheet, handouts

Personal Experience Teaching Methods

1. Outreach visitation

2. Personal witnessing

3. Ministry project

4. Fellowship gathering

5. Mentoring

6. Games

    Bible baseball

    Bible football

    Bible Jeopardy®

    Bible Linko®

    Bible word games

    Board games

    Clothespin Bible verse

Concentration
Scrambled verse
Secret codes
Simulation games
Sorting games
Spin and go
String-a-match
Surprise picture
Throw-catch-answer
Tic-tac-toe

Verbal/Auditory Teaching Methods
1. Brainstorming
2. Buzz Groups
3. Case studies
4. Circle response
5. Conversation
6. Debate
7. Discussion
8. Forum
9. Free association
10. Interview
11. Interview-report
12. Lecture
13. Listening teams
14. Memorization
15. Open-ended case study
16. Panel
17. Personal experience (share)
18. Problem solving
19. Problem-Issue research
20. Pro-Con analysis
21. Question and answer
22. Reaction panel
23. Research report
24. Resource persons

25. Retelling and resequencing
26. Storytelling
27. Study teams
28. Testimony
29. Testing
30. Word association
31. Written response(s)

Visual Teaching Methods

1. Non-projected visual
   Learning center
   Poster
   Objects, models
2. Projected visual
   Computer-generated
   Films
   Overhead projector
   Shadow puppet show
   Slides
   Video conferencing
   Videos
   PowerPoint® presentation

Terms to Avoid When Teaching

1. Ambiguous Designations
   "all of this"
   "and things"
   "somewhere"
   "other people"
2. Negated Intensifiers
   "not all"
   "not many"
   "not very"
3. Approximation
   "about as"
   "almost"

"pretty much"
4. "Bluffing" and Recovery
    "a long story short"
    "anyway"
    "as you all know"
    "of course"
5. Error Admission
    "excuse me"
    "not sure"
    "maybe I made an error"
    "I could be wrong"
6. Indeterminate Quantification
    "a bunch"
    "a couple"
    "few"
    "some"
7. Multiplicity
    "aspects"
    "factors"
    "sorts"
    "kinds"
8. Possibility
    "may"
    "might"
    "chances are"
    "could be"
9. Probability
    "probably"
    "sometimes"
    "ordinarily"
    "often"
    "frequently"

Tools of the Trade

Budgeting Guidelines

1. Plan
   - Plan consistently with church policies.
   - Plan in consideration of current conditions and situation plus vision for future.
   - Plan to include both long-range and short-range considerations.
2. Program
   - Make programs detailed and time-phased.
   - Connect programs to the mission of the church.
   - Tailor budget to mission and programming.
   - Begin budgeting process early (5-6 months before fiscal year).
   - Gather information: maintenance, development, staffing, and ministry and program budget needs.
   - Receive budget requests and compile them into a preliminary budget.
   - Finance or Stewardship Committee finalizes budget and recommends to congregation for adoption.
   - Call a business meeting budget adoption by congregation.
3. Control
   - Monitor budget expenditures.
   - Monitor giving patterns:
     Normal giving base: 1/3 of members give 2/3 of budget (the "20/80" rule)
     Cautionary giving base: 1/4 of members give 3/4 of budget
     Dangerous giving base: 1/5 of members give 4/5 of budget
   - Publish monthly financial reports.
   - Provide financial statements for individual givers.
   - Provide for audits as appropriate.

Copyright Myths

Copyright laws are complex. The following common myths may serve as a cautionary guide:

Myth 1. If a work doesn't have a copyright symbol, it is not copyrighted.

FACT: A copyright notice is optional. A work is considered copyrighted once it is produced, regardless of whether the author or creator includes the copyright notice.

Myth 2. Giving credit for a work quoted or cited means you don't have to ask permission.

FACT: Giving credit does not mean you've not violated the copyrights of the author or creator of a work. If in doubt, ask permission to use the work or a portion of it.

Myth 3. Quoting less than three sentences of a work or a few bars of a musical piece does not require permission.

FACT: The rules of "fair use" are fuzzy. Quoting three sentences from an 800-page book may be fair use, but three sentences from a work of poetry usually is not. Quantity is a poor rule when it comes to copyrights—if in doubt, ask permission.

Myth 4. Adapting, revising, expanding, or rewriting a work changes it enough not to require permission.

FACT: Copyrights extend to modifications of works.

Myth 5. Using a work that is in the public domain does not require permission.

FACT: Maybe, maybe not. Some things not covered under copyrights are covered under trademark restrictions. If in doubt, ask permission.

Myth 6. Content found on the Internet and posted anonymously is in the public domain and not copyrighted.

FACT: Material posted on the Internet without the author's or creator's permission may be a copyright infringement. Just because you cannot determine who the author is does not mean you can use it without discretion.

Myth 7. If one cannot track down the author, creator, or copyright holder after a bona fide attempt to obtain permission, the work can be used or quoted in good conscience.

FACT: Authors and creators of works have the right to refuse you the use of their work. Trying to get permission "after the fact" often has dire consequences.

Myth 8. Material found in books that are out of print can be considered in the public domain and therefore do not require permission.

FACT: When a book goes out of print it does not go into the public domain; the copyrights usually revert back to the author.

Myth 9. Material used for educational purposes falls under "fair use" and does not require permission.

FACT: Educational fair use is fuzzy, but there are guidelines about what constitutes fair use in relation to context, purpose, nature of the work, amount of the work used, etc. Check with your institution's guidelines.

Myth 10. If a work is more than seventy-five years old, the copyright has expired; permission is not needed to use it.

FACT: Works seventy-five years old and older may still be protected under ever-expanding copyright laws. In addition, international copyrights may extend the protection of the work. So the best advice is always to ask permission! Check the U.S. Copyright Office website for more information: http://lcweb.loc.gov/copyright/.

Dewey Decimal Classification for Christian Education

268 Religious Education

    .01 Functions, Aims

    .03 Encyclopedias and Dictionaries

    .05 Magazines, Periodicals, Journals

    .07 Religious Education and Public Schools; Government

    .09 History of Religious Education

.1 Administration

    .12 Constitution and By-laws

    .14 Business

        .142 Finances

.2 Buildings and Equipment

    .21 Grounds

    .22 Buildings

    .23 Plan and Arrangement of Rooms

        .231 Administrative Rooms & Offices

        .232 Study, Lecture, and Classrooms

        .233 Library, Resource Center, Museum

        .234 Manual Work Rooms

        .235 Social Rooms

        .236 Gymnasium

        .237 Sanitation, Lavatories

        .239 Accessories

    .24 Furnishings; Decorating

        .241 Furniture and Fixtures

.3 Personnel

    .32 Trustees, Directors, etc.

    .33 Administration, Supervision

        .332 Pastor, Associate Pastor

        .333 Superintendent

        .334 Administrative Assistants

            .3334 Clerk

            .3345 Custodian

        .335 Treasurer

        .336 Librarian

.337 Chorister, Musicians

.339 Other

.34 Committees

.37 Teachers

    .371 Qualifications

    .372 Training

        .3721 Training Workshops

        .3722 Manuals and Handbooks for Training

    .376 Promotion, Salary Scale

.38 Devotional Life

.4 Organization

.42 Membership

.43 Teaching Departments

    .432 Children's Division

        .4321 Cradle Roll

        .4322 Nursery, Crib Babies

        .4323 Kindergarten

    .433 Youth Division

        .4331 Junior High

        .4332 Senior High

    .434 Adult Division

    .435 Home Groups

    .436 Distance Learning, Correspondence Courses

    .437 Special Classes or Schools

        .4371 Kindergarten (weekday)

        .4373 Bible Clubs

        .4374 Vacation Bible School

        .4376 Camp and Conferences

        .4378 Bible Schools, Colleges, Seminaries

        .4379 Other

.44 Graded School

.45 Scholarship Records, Record-keeping Systems

.46 Examinations, Tests, Promotions

.47 Certificates, Diplomas

.48 Outside Activities

    .481 Sports and Games

.5 Records and Rules
    .51 Rules
    .52 Attendance, Tardiness, Absences
    .55 Vacation
.6 Materials and Methods of Instruction
    .61 Lesson Systems
    .62 Textbook Method
    .63 Lecture Method
        .631 Children's Stories
        .635 Visual Instruction (visual aids)
    .65 Question and Answer Method, Discussion
    .67 Drama (biblical)
    .68 Manual Work
    .69 Other Methods
.7 Sunday School Support Services
.8 Religious Education in Various Denominations
.9 Special Interest Areas

HTML Codes for Web-page Design

Basic Formating:
For bold type: **text within tags will be bold**
For italics: <i>*text within tags will be italicized*</i>
For underline: <u>text within tags will be underlined</u>
New paragraph: <p>
Line break:
Heading sizes: <h1>biggest</h1> to <h6>smallest</h6>

Listing Formats:
Numbered list
    <ol> (this tag opens the "ordered list")
    <li>First line item
    <li>Second line item
    <li>etc. . . .
    </ol> (this tag closes the ordered list)
Bulleted list
    <ul> (this tag opens the "unordered list")

<li>First bulleted line
<li>Second bulleted line
<li>etc. . . .
</ul> (this tag closes the unordered list)
Definition list
    <dl> (this tag opens the "definition list")
    <dt>First term
    <dd>First definition
    <dt>Second term
    <dd>Second definition
    etc. . . . .
    </dl> (this tag closes the definition list)

Navigational Links Tags
External link: <A HREF="URL">link text</a>
Anchor: <A NAME="Anchor name">link text</a>
Internal link: <A HREF="#Anchor name">link text</a>
E-mail link: <A HREF=mailto:emailaddress@here>link text</a>.

Miscellaneous

Canonical Hours

Matins with lauds (midnight or 2 A.M., but also at sunrise)
Prime (first hour of the day)
Tierce (third hour after sunrise)
Sext (sixth hour of the day or noon)
Nones (ninth hour after sunrise)
Vespers (late afternoon or evening)
Compline (just before retiring for the day)

Christian Church Year

Advent Season
    First Sunday in Advent
    Second Sunday in Advent
    Third Sunday in Advent
    Fourth Sunday in Advent
Christmas Season
    Christmas Eve (December 24)
    Christmas Day (December 25)
    Christmastide (Sunday after Christmas)
    New Year's Eve
    New Year's Day
Epiphany (January 6)
    First Sunday in Epiphany
    Second Sunday in Epiphany
    Third Sunday in Epiphany
    Fourth Sunday in Epiphany
    Fifth Sunday in Epiphany

Sixth Sunday in Epiphany
Septuagesima
Sexagesima
Quinquagesima
Lenten Season
   Ash Wednesday (February or March)
   First Sunday in Lent: Invocavit
   Second Sunday in Lent: *Reminiscere*
   Third Sunday in Lent: *Oculi*
   Fourth Sunday in Lent: *Laetare*
   Fifth Sunday in Lent: *Judica*
   Holy Week (March or April)
   Palm Sunday
   Maundy Thursday
   Good Friday
Easter (March or April)
   Eastertide (Sundays after Easter)
Pentecost (April or May)
Trinity Sunday (May or June)
All Saint's Eve (October 31)
Reformation Sunday (October 31)
All Saint's Day (November 1)

Denominations in the U.S. (Major)

Anglican
Baptist
Church of Christ
Congregational
Eastern Orthodox
Episcopalian
Evangelical
Fundamentalist Independent
Greek Orthodox
Lutheran
Mennonite
Methodist

Moravian
Pentecostal
Presbyterian
Quaker
Roman Catholic
Russian Orthodox
Salvation Army

Five Cardinal Virtues

1. Benevolence
2. Duty
3. Manners
4. Wisdom
5. Faithfulness

Five Points of Calvinism

1. Total Depravity
2. Unconditional Election
3. Limited Atonement
4. Irresistible Grace
5. Perseverance of the Saints

Music

Hymns (Popular)

"Abide with Me: Fast Falls the Eventide"
"Abide with Us through All the Coming Years"
"All Hail the Power of Jesus' Name"
"All Heaven Declares the Glory of the Risen Lord"
"All People That on Earth Do Dwell"
"All Things Bright and Beautiful"
"Amazing Grace! How Sweet the Sound"
"And Did Those Feet in Ancient Time"
"Ave, Maria, Gratia Plena"
"Be Thou My Vision, O Lord of My Heart"
"Blessed Assurance, Jesus Is Mine!"
"Come Thou Fount of Every Blessing"

"Crown Him with Many Crowns"

"Dear Lord and Father of Mankind"

"For the Beauty of the Earth"

"God of All Living"

"Great Is Thy Faithfulness"

"Guide Me, O Thou Great Jehovah"

"Holy, Holy, Holy"

"How Lovely Is Thy Dwelling-Place"

"I Am Weak but Thou Art Strong"

"I Stand Amazed in the Presence of Jesus the Nazarene"

"I Want to Walk With Jesus Christ"

"Immortal, Invisible, God Only Wise"

"Isn't the Love of Jesus Something Wonderful"

"It Is Well with My Soul"

"Jesus Loves Me, This I Know"

"Jesus, the Very Thought of Thee"

"Joyful, Joyful, We Adore Thee"

"Love Divine, All Loves Excelling"

"Morning Has Broken Like the First Morning"

"My Hope Is Built on Nothing Less"

"My Jesus, I Love Thee, I Know Thou Art Mine"

"Now Thank We All Our God"

"O For a Thousand Tongues to Sing"

"O Jesus, I Have Promised"

"O Lord My God! When I in Awesome Wonder"

"O Perfect Love, All Human Thought Transcending"

"O Worship the King All Glorious Above"

"Praise to the Lord, the Almighty, the King"

"Savior Like a Shepherd Lead Us"

"Tell Me the Old, Old Story"

"The King of Love My Shepherd Is"

"The Lord's My Shepherd, I'll Not Want"

"The Solid Rock"

"To God Be the Glory! Great Things He Hath Done"

"Trust and Obey! For There's No Other Way"

"What a Fellowship, What a Joy Divine"

"What a Friend We Have in Jesus"
"When I Survey the Wondrous Cross"
"When We Walk with the Lord"
"Worship the King All Glorious Above"
"You Who Dwell in the Shelter of the Lord"

Praise Choruses (Popular)

"Ah, Lord God"
"All Hail King Jesus"
"Alleluia"
"All Heav'n Declares"
"Almighty"
"Ancient of Days"
"As the Deer"
"Awesome God"
"Awesome in this Place"
"Be Exalted"
"Because He Lives"
"Before the Throne of God"
"Bind Us Together"
"Bless His Holy Name"
"Blessed Be the Lord God"
"Blessed Be the Name of the Lord"
"Celebrate Jesus"
"Change My Heart, Oh God"
"Come Let Us Worship and Bow Down"
"Emmanuel"
"Father I Adore You"
"Garment of Praise"
"Give Thanks"
"Glorify Thy Name"
"God Will Make a Way"
"Great and Mighty"
"Great Is the Lord"
"He Is Exalted"
"He Who Began a Good Work in You"

"He Will Come and Save You"
"His Name Is Wonderful"
"Holy Ground"
"Holy Spirit, Thou Art Welcome"
"Holy, Holy"
"Holy, Holy, Holy"
"Hosanna"
"How Deep Is the Father's Love for Us"
"How Great Thou Art"
"How Majestic Is Your Name"
"I Could Sing of Your Love Forever"
"I Exalt Thee"
"I Love You with the Love of the Lord"
"I Love You, Lord"
"I Offer My Life"
"I Sing Praises to Your Name"
"I Stand in Awe"
"I Want to Be Where You Are"
"I Will Bless the Lord"
"I Will Call Upon the Lord"
"I Will Enter"
"I Will Seek Your Face"
"I'm Forever Grateful"
"In Him We Live"
"In His Time"
"In Moments Like These"
"In the Presence of Jehovah"
"Isn't He?"
"Jesus, Lord to Me"
"Jesus, Lover of My Soul (It's All about You)"
"Jesus, Name Above All Names"
"King of Kings"
"Lamb of God"
"Lead Me, Lord"
"Let Everything That Has Breath"
"Let It Rise"

"Let the Redeemed of the Lord Say So"
"Let There Be Glory and Honor and Praises"
"Let's Just Praise the Lord"
"Lift Up Your Heads"
"Lord, Be Glorified"
"Lord, I Lift Your Name on High"
"Lord, You Are So Precious to Me"
"Majesty"
"Make Us One"
"Mighty Is Our God"
"More Precious Than Silver"
"My Tribute"
"O How He Loves You and Me"
"O Lord, You're Beautiful"
"O the Glory of Your Presence"
"Once Again"
"Open Our Eyes, Lord"
"Our God Reigns"
"People Need the Lord"
"People of God"
"Praise the Name of Jesus"
"Praise You"
"Sanctuary"
"Seek Ye First"
"Shine, Jesus, Shine"
"Shout to the Lord"
"Sing Hallelujah to the Lord"
"Something Beautiful"
"Soon and Very Soon"
"Spirit of the Living God"
"Surely the Presence of the Lord"
"Sweet, Sweet Spirit"
"The Battle Belongs to the Lord"
"The Bond of Love"
"The Family of God"
"The Greatest Thing"

"The River Is Here"
"The Steadfast Love of the Lord"
"The Trees of the Field"
"There Is a Redeemer"
"There's Something About That Name"
"This Is the Day"
"Thou Art Worthy"
"Through the Blood"
"Thy Loving Kindness"
"Thy Word"
"Turn Your Eyes Upon Jesus"
"Victory Chant"
"We Are an Offering"
"We Bow Down"
"We Bring a Sacrifice"
"We Declare Your Majesty"
"We Have Come into His House"
"We Will Glorify"
"What a Mighty God"
"When I Look into Your Holiness"
"Where the Spirit of the Lord Is"
"Who Paints the Skies (River of Fire)"
"Worthy, You Are Worthy"
"Yes, Lord, Yes"
"You Are All I Need"
"You Are My All in All"
"You Are My Hiding Place"
"You Are Worthy"
"(You Turned My) Mourning into Dancing"
"Your Love Is My Everlasting"

Pledges

Pledge to the American Flag
I pledge allegiance to the flag
Of the United States of America,
And to the Republic for which it stands.

One nation, under God, indivisible,
With liberty and justice for all.

Pledge to the Christian Flag
I pledge allegiance to the Christian flag
And to the Savior for whose kingdom it stands.
One brotherhood, united for all mankind,
In service and in love.

Pledge to the Bible
I pledge allegiance to the Bible,
God's holy word.
I will make it a lamp unto my feet,
And a light unto my path.
I will hide its words in my heart,
that I might not sin against God.

Seven Deadly Sins
1. Pride
2. Covetousness
3. Lust
4. Anger
5. Gluttony
6. Envy
7. Sloth

Seven Roman Catholic Sacraments
Baptism
Confirmation
Eucharist
Confession (Penance)
Holy Orders
Marriage
Anointing the Sick

Seven Spiritual Works

1. Convert the sinner.
2. Instruct the ignorant.
3. Counsel the doubtful.
4. Comfort the sorrowing.
5. Bear wrongs patiently.
6. Forgive injuries.
7. Pray for the living and the dead.

Seven Works of Mercy

1. Feed the hungry.
2. Give drink to the thirsty.
3. Harbor the stranger.
4. Clothe the naked.
5. Tend the sick.
6. Minister to prisoners.
7. Bury the dead.

Stages of Grief

Elizabeth Kübler-Ross identified the stages of grief in the dying process as:

1. denial and isolation
2. anger
3. bargaining
4. depression
5. acceptance

Symbols of Christianity

Alpha-Omega (eternality of Christ)
Anchor (faith)
Bread and Wine (eucharist — death of Christ)
Chi-Rho (first two letters of "Christ" in Greek)
Cross (death of Christ)
Dove (Holy Spirit at baptism of Christ)
Fire (Holy Spirit on Day of Pentecost)

Fish (initial letters of "Jesus Christ, God's Son, Savior" in Greek,
    spelling ICHTHUS, the Greek word for "fish")
Lamb (Christ's self-sacrifice)
Shepherd (Christ's care for his people)
Ship (Church)
Vine (Christ's union with his people; wine of eucharist)

Wedding Anniversary Years and Gifts

1. Paper (plastic); cotton; clocks
2. Cotton (calico); paper; china
3. Leather; crystal; glass
4. Linen; iron; appliances; fruit; flowers
5. Wood; silverware
6. Iron; sugar; wood
7. Wool; copper or brass; desk set
8. Bronze; linens; lace
9. Pottery or china; copper; leather
10. Tin; diamond
11. Steel; fashion jewelry
12. Silk or fine linen; pearl; colored gems
13. Lace; textile; furs
14. Gold jewelry
15. Crystal; watches
20. China; platinum
25. Silver; sterling silver
30. Pearl; diamond
35. Coral or jade
40. Ruby
45. Sapphire
50. Gold
55. Emerald
60. Diamond; gold
70. Platinum

Bibliography

Ausubel, David. *Educational Psychology: A Cognitive View.* New York: Holt, Rinehart & Winston, Inc., 1968.

Bloom, Benjamin S. (ed.) *Taxonomy of Educational Objectives: Handbook I: Cognitive Domain.* New York: David McKay Company, Inc., 1956.

———. *Taxonomy of Educational Objectives: Handbook II: Affective Domain.* New York: David McKay Company, Inc., 1964

Bruner, Jerome S. *The Process of Education.* Cambridge MA: Harvard University Press, 1960.

Charpentier, Etienne. *How to Read the New Testament.* New York: Crossroad Publishing Co., 1990.

———. *How to Read the Old Testament.* New York: Crossroad, Publishing Co., 1992.

Cross, Patricia K. *Adults as Learners.* San Francisco: Jossey-Bass Publishers, 1981.

Dewey, Melvil. *Dewey Decimal Classification and Relative Index.* Eighth Abridged Edition. New York: Forest Press, Inc.,1965.

Dick, Walter, and Lou Me Carey. *The Systematic Design of Instruction.* New York: Addison Wesley Publishing Co., 1996.

Duke, Michael Hare. *Freud.* Makers of Modern Thought Series, ed. A. D. Galloway. Valley Forge: Judson Press, 1972.

Erikson, Erik H. *Childhood and Society.* Second edition. New York: W. W. Norton & Co., Inc., 1963.

Fowler, James. *Stages of Faith.* New York: Harper & Row, 1981.

Freud, S. *An Outline of Psychoanalysis.* London: Hogarth, 1973.

Gagne, Robert. *Principles of Instructional Design.* New York: Holt, Rinehart & Winston, 1979.

Galindo, Israel. *The Craft of Christian Teaching.* Valley Forge: Judson Press, 1998.

Gardner, Howard. *Frames of Mind: The Theory of Multiple Intelligences.* New York: Basic Books, 1995.

Hannafin, Michael J., and Kyle L. Peck. *The Design Development and Evaluation of Instructional Software.* Englewood Cliff, NJ: Prentice-Hall Publishers, 1997.

Harrison, Everett F. *Introduction to the New Testament.* Revised edition. Grand Rapids: Wm. B. Eerdmans Publishing Co., 1971.

Havighurst, Robert J. *Developmental Tasks for Education.* New York: David McKay Co., 1972.

Kerr, Michael E., and Murray Bowen. *Family Evaluation.* New York: W. W. Norton & Co., 1988.

Kipfer, Barbara Ann. *The Order of Things.* New York: Random House, 1997.

Kirkpatric, Donald. *Evaluating Training Programs.* San Francisco:Berrett-Koehler, 1998.

Knowles, Malcolm S. *The Modern Practice of Adult Education.* New York: Association Press, 1979.

Kohlberg, Lawrence. *The Psychology of Moral Development.* New York: Harper & Row, Publishers, 1983.

Kolb, David. *Experiential Learning: Experience as the Source of Learning and Development.* Englewood Cliffs NJ: Prentice-Hall, 1984.

Kübler-Ross, Elizabeth. *On Death and Dying.* New York: Tavistock Publications, 1969.

Lewis, Michael. ed. *Origins of Intelligence: Infancy and Early Childhood.* Second edition. New York: Plenum Press, 1983.

Maslow, Abraham H. *Motivation and Personality.* Second edition. New York: Harper & Row Publishers, 1970.

Mayr, Marlene, ed. *Modern Masters of Christian Education.* Birmingham AL: Religious Education Press, 1983.

Nelson's Complete Book of Bible Maps & Charts: Old and New Testaments. Nashville: Thomas Nelson Publishers, 1982.

Oswald, Roy M., and Robert E. Friedrich Jr. *Discerning Your Congregation's Future.* An Alban Institute Publication, 1966.

Packer, J. I. et al. *Nelson's Illustrated Encyclopedia of Bible Facts.* Nashville: Thomas Nelson Publishers, 1980.

Piaget, Jean. *Six Psychological Studies.* New York: Random House, 1967.

Powers, Bruce P., ed. *Christian Education Handbook.* Nashville: Broadman Press, 1981.

————. *Church Administration Handbook*. Nashville: Broadman Press, 1981.

Rogers, Carl. *Freedom to Learn*. Columbus OH: Charles E. Merrill Publishing Co., 1969.

Rohr, Richard and Andreas Ebert. *Discovering the Enneagram*. New York: Crossroad, 1991.

Rothauge, Arlin J. *Sizing Up a Congregation*. New York: Episcopal Church Center, 1985.

Seymour, Jack L., ed. *Mapping Christian Education*. Nashville: Abingdon Press, 1997.

Skinner, B. F. *Science and Human Behavior*. New York: The MacMillan Company, 1953.

Thomas, R. Murray. *Comparing Theories of Child Development*. Belmont CA: Wadsworth Publishing Co., 1985.

Tye, Karen B. *Basics of Christian Education*. St. Louis MO: Chalice Press, 2000.

Vigotsky, L. S. *Thought and Language*. Cambridge MA: M.I.T. Press, 1962.

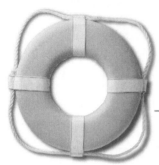